THE BRIDGESTONE
100 BEST RESTAURANTS IN IRELAND 2002

GW00713187

THE BRIDGESTONE

100 BEST
RESTAURANTS
IN IRELAND 2002

JOHN McKENNA - SALLY McKENNA

ESTRAGON PRESS

FIRST PUBLISHED IN 2002

BY ESTRAGON PRESS

DURRUS

COUNTY CORK

© ESTRAGON PRESS

TEXT © JOHN & SALLY McKENNA

THE MORAL RIGHT OF THE AUTHORS

HAS BEEN ASSERTED

ISBN 1 874076 43 X

PRINTED IN SPAIN BY GRAPHYCEMS

WRITTEN BY JOHN McKENNA

CONTRIBUTING EDITORS:

ORLA BRODERICK

ELIZABETH FIELD

CAROLINE WORKMAN

PUBLISHING EDITOR: SALLY McKENNA

EDITOR: JUDITH CASEY

ART DIRECTION BY NICK CANN

COVER PHOTOS BY MIKE O'TOOLE

ILLUSTRATIONS BY AOIFE WASSER

WEB: FLUIDEDGE.IE

FOR
TOBY SIMMONDS

WITH THANKS TO...

Colm Conyngham, Des Collins, Brian Condon,

Claire Goodwillie, Frieda Forde,

Sile Ginnane, Conor Cahill,

Judith Casey, Maureen Daly,

Nick Cann, Pat Young,

Margie Deverell, Lelia McKenna,

Mike O'Toole, Ann Marie Tobin

Leslie Williams, Josette Cadoret

BRIDGESTONE TYRES

...is the world's largest tyre and rubber manufacturer.

■ Founded in Japan in 1931, it currently employs over 95,000 people in Europe, Asia and America and its products are sold in more than 150 countries. Its European plants are situated in France, Spain and Italy.

■ Bridgestone manufacture tyres for a wide variety of vehicles from passenger cars and motorcycles, trucks and buses to giant earthmovers and aircraft.

■ Many Japanese and European cars sold in Ireland have been fitted with Bridgestone tyres during manufacture and a host of exotic sports cars, including Ferrari, Lamborghini, Porsche and Jaguar, are fitted with Bridgestone performance tyres as original equipment.

■ Bridgestone commercial vehicle tyres enjoy a worldwide reputation for superior cost per kilometre performance and its aircraft tyres are used by more than 100 airlines.

■ In 1988 Bridgestone acquired the Firestone Tyre and Rubber Company combining the resources of both companies under one umbrella. This, coupled with an intensive research and development programme, has enabled Bridgestone to remain the world's most technologically advanced tyre company with testing centres in Japan, USA, Mexico and Italy.

■ Bridgestone tyres are distributed in Ireland by Bridgestone/Firestone Ireland Limited, a subsidiary of the multinational Bridgestone Corporation. A wide range of tyres are stocked in its central warehouse and staff provide sales, technical and delivery services all over Ireland.

■ Bridgestone tyres are available from tyre dealers throughout Ireland.

FOR FURTHER INFORMATION:

BRIDGESTONE/FIRESTONE IRELAND LTD
Unit 4
Leopardstown Office Park,
Dublin 18
Tel: (01) 295 2844
Fax: (01) 295 2858

34 Hillsborough Road,
Lisburn
BT28 1AQ
Tel: 028 926 78331

website: www.bridgestone-eu.com

• It used to be a relatively simple annual matter, collating and describing the 100 best restaurants in Ireland. Of course, there was always a certain amount of teeth grinding as one got down to the very last few places to be included, and a fair amount of debate as to who merited inclusion and who didn't.

• Well, it's gotten a whole lot more complex nowadays, as our team of editors line up and argue the toss for the places they rate, and decry the places they don't rate at all, thanks very much. There is lots of discussion, and more than a little argument.

• This is a very healthy state of affairs, of course, and one we enjoy. Decisions on who is relevant and what is significant in Ireland's restaurant culture are not a closed book. Like any part of our culture, it is an issue to be debated, and one where disagreement is healthy. We have moved a long way from the days when guidebooks would issue their writ, and expect it to be treated with catechism-like conformity.

• But, in the middle of the argument, what we always try to avoid is any committee-like behaviour, where special pleading and politics have more effect than true criticism. We hope that the Bridgestone Guides reflect a team effort, where diverse opinions gather to elect the best, in all its resplendent brilliance.

John & Sally McKenna
Durrus, West Cork, March 2002

"Dictionaries therefore bring gravity to matters that are elusive, frivolous, or forever in a state of metamorphosis"

– A Biographical Dictionary of Film, David Thomson

• Defining good food is simple, but guidebooks have traditionally muddied the simplicity. They try to forget the elusiveness and frivolity of great cooking, and they imagine that one can ignore that food and its makers are forever in a state of metamorphosis.

• But great cooking is a fleeting thing. To take a quote from the food writer, Annie Bell, we find it in "the instant of its perfection". And when we find it, we all know just what it is. You don't have to be a critic to know it: you just have to be an appreciative customer.

• Appreciative customers will, therefore, disagree with our Bridgestone awards, and that is the way it should be.

a classic

worth a detour

an icon

Our icons might be your iconoclasts, our detours might not persuade you to pull off the road, and our classics might be your idea of a jalopy. But we have chosen these awards as best representing the individual spirit of the entry to whom they are given. With our icons, we are searching for cooks who are utterly of the moment, people whose food creates new paradigms of pleasure.

• For those we reckon worthy of a detour, there is an excitement and challenge about their work that heralds great promise. And our classics are people who – to borrow a line from Leonard Cohen – understand "the simplicities of pleasure". And pleasure is always a simple thing, as simple as defining good food.

icons

Alden's, Belfast

Café Paradiso, Cork

Cayenne, Belfast

The Commons, Dublin

The Customs House, Baltimore

Restaurant Michael Deane, Belfast

L'Ecrivain, Dublin

Fishy Fishy Café, Kinsale

Island Cottage, Heir Island

Longueville House, Mallow

MacNean Bistro, Cavan

La Marine, Rosslare

Mermaid Café, Dublin

Packie's, Kenmare

Shanks, Bangor

The Tannery, Dungarvan

Thorntons, Dublin

classic

Allo's Bar & Bistro, Listowel

Ballymore Inn, Ballymore Eustace

Brocka-on-the-Water, Kilgarvan Quay

Buggy's Glencairn Inn, Glencairn

The Corncrake, Carndonagh

Halo, Dublin

Jacob's on the Mall, Cork

Jacques, Cork

O'Callaghan-Walshe, Rosscarbery

Richmond House, Cappoquin

Roly's Bistro, Dublin

Sheen Falls Lodge, Kenmare

The Strawberry Tree, Macreddin

Sun Kee, Belfast

The Tea Room, Dublin

detour

Avoca Handweavers, Kilmacanogue

Belfast Bar & Grill, Belfast

Caviston's, Dublin

Chapter One, Dublin

The Chart House, Dingle

Cherry Tree Restaurant, Killaloe

The Cross of Cloyne, Midleton

Fontana, Holywood

Ginger, Belfast

High Moors, Clifden

Left Bank Bistro, Athlone

Legends Restaurant, Cashel

The Mermaid, Liscannor

Nimmo's, Galway

Restaurant David Norris, Tralee

One Pico, Dublin

Otto's Creative Cuisine, Dunworley

Powersfield House, Dungarvan

The Water Margin, Belfast

• The Bridgestone 100 Best Restaurants in Ireland is arranged **ALPHABETICALLY, BY COUNTY** so it begins with County Cavan, which is followed by County Clare, and so on.

• Within the counties, the entries are once again listed alphabetically by name, so Flappers, Tulla, south Clare, is followed by The Mermaid, Liscannor, north Clare.

• Entries in Northern Ireland are listed alphabetically, at the end of the book. NI prices are quoted in pounds sterling.

• The contents of the Bridgestone 100 Best Guides are exclusively the result of the editors' deliberations. All meals and accommodation were paid for and any offers of discounts or gifts were refused.

• Many of the places featured in this book are only open during the summer season, which means that they can be closed for any given length of time between October and March. Many others change their opening times during the winter.

• **PRICES:** Dinner prices are calculated for an average three course menu, without wine. Where the restaurant operates a set menu, that price is given. All prices and details are correct at the time of going to press.

• **CREDIT CARDS:** Most restaurants take major credit cards, particularly the Visa, Access/Master group. If a restaurant does not accept credit cards, this is indicated in the notes section of their entry.

• Finally, we greatly appreciate receiving reports, suggestions and criticisms from readers, and would like to thank those who have written in the past, whose opinions are of enormous assistance to us when considering which 100 restaurants finally make it into this book.

CONTENTS

MacNEAN BISTRO

The Maguire family
MacNean Bistro
Blacklion,
Co Cavan
Tel: (072) 53022
Fax: (072) 53404

Neven Maguire's brilliant
cooking has made Blacklion
a gourmet grotto.

A youthful twenty-something with a perennial grin, Neven Maguire is a virtuoso of the kitchen. His appreciation for the superlative artisan foods he has on his doorstep leads to great cooking where the chef finds his own signature in the search for outstanding flavours; Thornhill duckling is made into confit and served with a spring roll of the confit and red cabbage with 5-spice; west coast hake is paired with scallops, saffron orzo and a lobster cream; local organic vegetables and salad leaves shine with every dish. If the savoury cooking is special, the sweet cooking is spectacular: Maguire is the finest dessert chef in the country. Pineapple and polenta upside-down cake has a tongue-teasing coconut parfait; a warm soft chocolate cake with white chocolate and poached cherries is so voluptuous and sexy as to verge on the indecent. Irresistible. The newly redesigned room is simply delightful, and a perfect stage for extraordinary talent.

- **OPEN:** 6pm-9pm Tue-Sun, 1pm & 3.15pm Sun
- **PRICE:** Lunch €20, Dinner €42, House wine €17.95
- **CREDIT CARDS:** Visa, Mastercard

- **NOTES:**
Wheelchair access.
Children – welcome, high chair, half portions.
Recommended for vegetarians, special menu.

- **DIRECTIONS:**
On the main street in Blacklion, which itself is just on the border with Northern Ireland.

BARRTRÁ

Paul & Theresa O'Brien
Barrtrá Seafood Restaurant,
Barrtrá,
Lahinch,
Co Clare
Tel: (065) 708 1280

One of the quintessential simple,
seaside, holiday-time restaurants,
with relaxed, mature seafood cookery
and great service.

It's not easy to write a critique of Paul and Theresa
O'Brien's Barrtrá. What they do, and the way they do it,
is so organic and simple and logical that the realms of
criticism are rendered virtually redundant. Who needs
critics when food is produced, prepared and served in the
time-honoured way that this couple have been doing for
more than ten years?

So, criticism must yield to praise for their appreciation of
fresh fish and shellfish, their production of their own
vegetables in the garden, and the solicitous care with
which this food is cooked and served, and indeed,
matched with interesting wines. You sit in this simple
dining room, enjoying dinner, casting an eye over the
enchanting view of Liscannor Bay, and all is well with the
world. And isn't that just what restaurants are supposed
to be all about? Well, in our book, it is.

● **OPEN:** 5pm-10pm Tue-Sun (closed Nov-Jan, open 7
days high season)
● **PRICE:** Dinner €33, House wine €12.50
● **CREDIT CARDS:** Visa, Mastercard, Amex

● **NOTES:**
Reservations recommended. Wheelchair access (but not
to toilets). Children – early evening only. Recommended
for vegetarians.

● **DIRECTIONS:**
Signposted from the Milton Malbay/Lahinch road, and
from the main street in Lahinch.

CHERRY TREE RESTAURANT

Harry McKeogh
Lakeside, Ballina,
Killaloe,
Co Clare
Tel: (061) 375688,
Fax: (061) 375689

A philosophical, wise kitchen, with fine food from a fired-up team under Harry McKeogh.

Harry McKeogh makes it look easy. Build a restaurant from scratch. Hire a great local team in the kitchen and out front. Produce delicious food at excellent prices. Send everyone home happy. Not a bother on the man at all. And he really does make it all seem so straightforward. The Cherry Tree food is so delicious, so logical and wise, with local foods everywhere: Glenarm salmon with vodka crème fraîche; Roundstone hake with cornmeal and buttermilk fried oysters; Bluebell Falls goat's cheese on crostini; Castletown crabmeat spring rolls; dry-aged Tipperary beef. This kitchen has thought long and hard about what it wants to do, and does things exactly as they want. "Good food depends entirely on good ingredients", they write on the menu, and with ceaseless energy they put this into practice every day, a perfect unity of philosophy and skill producing fabulous food.

● **OPEN:** 6pm-10pm Tue-Sat, 6pm-10pm Sun & Bank hols
● **PRICE:** Dinner €38, House wine €17.20
● **CREDIT CARDS:** Visa, Mastercard, Amex, Laser

● **NOTES:**
Recommended for vegetarians. Suitable for children over 7 years. Full wheelchair access.

● **DIRECTIONS:**
Turn off the N7 for Ballina/Killaloe, drive through Ballina village, turn left towards the bridge and right at Molly's pub, just before bridge, towards Lakeside Hotel.

FLAPPERS

**Patricia Cahill &
Jim McInerney
Main Street,
Tulla,
Co Clare
Tel: (065) 6835711**

Forget the renowned ceili band: Patricia Cahill's swish, smart restaurant is the real star of the sweet little town of Tulla.

Flappers is the sort of restaurant you could easily overlook. It's modest, understated, quiet: you could walk up the main street of Tulla and scarcely notice it.

But food lovers who appreciate cooking that shows ingenuity and a search for true flavour know all about Patricia Cahill and her simple restaurant. For here is a mighty cook: talented, determined, capable, with a woman's instinct for womanly cooking that comes through in a celebration of great flavours.

Staples such as roast rack of lamb with rosemary, or barbary duck with pork, or braised pheasant with whiskey, are handled with the aplomb of a chef with serious technique (Ms Cahill trained in the Culinary Institute of America), but overall it is the consolation of great country flavours that this food speaks of, with ace desserts to send you into the night singing with delight.

● **OPEN:** Noon-3pm Mon-Sat, 7pm-9.45pm Tue-Sat
(winter open noon-3pm Mon-Sat, 7pm-9.30pm Thur-Sat)
● **PRICE:** Lunch €10-13, Dinner €25-30, House wine €15.15
● **CREDIT CARDS:** Visa, Mastercard

● **NOTES:**
Wheelchair access.
Children welcome – high chair.

● **DIRECTIONS:**
Just across from the Courthouse in the centre of Tulla.

THE MERMAID

Kathi Marr & Neville Fitzpatrick
Liscannor Village,
Liscannor,
Co Clare
Tel: (065) 7081076
themermaid@ireland.com

Red-hot cooking from a kitchen delivering potent deliciousness with no-frills and lots of thrills.

The Mermaid is red-hot right now, a fabulous synthesis of Kathi Marr's great service and Neville Fitzpatrick's oh-my-God-it's-so-delicious cooking.

It's the simplest room you could imagine – all right, it redefines simplicity, it looks like a miniature call-centre – but the verve and alacrity of the atmosphere and the food is totally winning: signature dishes such as the superb crab Florentine (as good as it gets, quite frankly) or their baked sea bass with orange and spinach are utterly convincing, the swordfish with lime and pepper butter proof of how disciplined they can be. The mashed potato – which appears in a huge, whipped-up tower – gets our vote for the best mash in the country. Lovely salads, lovely desserts which include a truly great chocolate cake, great beers and wines, great sounds, and all in all the Mermaid is a demon restaurant.

- **OPEN:** 6pm-11pm Mon-Sun. Closed Nov-Mar
- **PRICE:** Dinner €35, House wine €17
- **CREDIT CARDS:** Visa, Mastercard

- **NOTES:**
Full wheelchair access. Children very welcome. Late night opening for tapas in high season - advertised locally. Booking advised for July and August.

- **DIRECTIONS:**
Leaving Liscannor village, heading towards the Cliffs of Moher, the Mermaid is immediately on the right, amongst a group of shops and a small car park.

AHERNE'S

The Fitzgibbon Family
Aherne's Seafood Restaurant,
163 Nth Main St, Youghal, Co Cork
Tel: (024) 92424, Fax: 93633
ahernes@eircom.net
www.ahernes.com

Boy, but the Fitzgibbon family make it look so easy to serve delicious food and offer splendid hospitality.

Aeons ago, John McKenna was a restaurant plongeur. Just as well he wasn't trying to get a gig in Aherne's, for the art of the dishwasher here is virtually superfluous in this east Cork institution. In the restaurant and the bar, the plates go back from the punters without a jot of food left on them, every iota eaten, mopped and enjoyed, so tasty is the work of David Fitzgibbon and his team.

They do much the same thing in Aherne's that they have always done; classic bourgeois fish cookery in the restaurant – sole on the bone; prawns in garlic butter; even old chargers such as sole with grapes – whilst there is snappy, enervated food in the bar – seafood pie; herb-crusted salmon with balsamic dressing; and excellent sandwiches and grills. It's a terrific mixture, and done with the consistency of the Fitzgibbon family, it never disappoints. Nice gig for the plongeur, too.

● **OPEN:** Restaurant open 6.30pm-9.30pm (bar food served from noon)
● **PRICE:** Dinner €38.10, House wine €18.50
● **CREDIT CARDS:** All major cards accepted

● **NOTES:**
Full wheelchair access.
Children welcome. Reservations advised for the restaurant.

● **DIRECTIONS:**
Just off the N25 road, which runs through the centre of Youghal. Well signposted from the road.

10 GREAT RESTAURANT
SIGNATURE DISHES

1

THE MERMAID, LISCANNOR
mashed potatoes

2

BELFAST BAR & GRILL
Irish stew

3

OTTO'S CREATIVE CATERING
wild salmon and monkfish with sea spinach

4

THE WATER MARGIN
mock chicken with cashew in bird's nest

5

RESTAURANT DAVID NORRIS
liquorice & lime parfait, pears & caramel

6

THE COMMONS
cannelloni of calves' sweetbreads, truffle jus

7

AN CARN
baked lemon tart

8

KEVIN ARUNDEL @ NUMBER 10
hot Carlingford oysters, fennel and mango

9

POWERSFIELD HOUSE
McGrath's fillet, onion marmalade & champ

10

AQUA
scallop salad with mango and chilli salsa

BALLYMALOE HOUSE

The Allen family
Shanagarry, Co Cork
Tel: (021) 465 2531,
Fax: 465 2029
res@ballymaloe.ie
www.ballymaloe.com

Myrtle Allen's Ballymaloe House is the great Irish modernist masterpiece, a unique oasis of civilised values.

"Oh, I never went in for any of that marketing talk," Myrtle Allen mentioned to us once. "I just tried to do the best I could and hoped someone would like it."
They liked it back in 1964, when Ballymaloe first opened, and they like it today, as Rory O'Connell, the chef, continues Mrs Allen's crusade for, simple, local, noble foods, cooked with sympathy and understanding. Today, the Ballymaloe team continues to do the best they can, from their gracious (and very understated) service, to the preparation of food with perspicacity and provenance. This is ageless cooking – a table of hors d'oeuvres to begin; wild watercress soup; chicken braised in Meursault; Cork kassler with peperonata; Cloyne beef with horseradish; Ballycotton plaice with herbed mayonnaise; superb Irish farmhouse cheeses – in an ageless house that remains just as much of a modernist masterpiece today as it was way back in 1964.

- **OPEN:** 1pm-1.30pm, 7pm-9.30pm Mon-Sun
- **PRICE:** Lunch €25, Dinner €55, House wine €21
- **CREDIT CARDS:** All major cards accepted

- **NOTES:**
Buffet lunch on Sunday 1pm, booking essential. Recommended for vegetarians, vegetarian table d'hote menu served every night. Wheelchair access with plenty of assistance. No children in dining room at dinner, otherwise children very welcome.

- **DIRECTIONS:**
18 miles east of Cork city. Take N25 to exit for Whitegate R630, follow signs for R629 Cloyne. House is 2 miles beyond Cloyne.

CAFÉ PARADISO

Denis Cotter & Bridget Healy
16 Lancaster Quay,
Cork, Co Cork
Tel: (021) 427 7939,
Fax: 427 4973
www.cafeparadiso.ie

Café Paradiso just has to be the finest vegetarian restaurant on the planet, right? Right.

Denis Cotter is one of the most original kitchen thinkers at work today, and Café Paradiso is one of the most original restaurants in the country.

What Denis Cotter and Bridget Healy have achieved over the last decade is awesome to consider. They have completely redefined "vegetarian" cooking, creating a vibrant, meat-free cuisine that, seemingly, has no antecedent. Of course, Mediterranean influences are evident in this cooking, but somehow they are so synthesised and absorbed that one can speak of a Café Paradiso cuisine that is sui generis. Out-of-the-box cookery, simple as that.

So, we'll have the wild rice and parsnip fritters with smoked cheese mash; the mangetout, chard and pinenut risotto; the couscous-crusted aubergine; the goat's cheese charlotte. Great wines, great service, unique place.

● **OPEN:** 12.30pm-3pm, 6.30pm-10.30pm Tue-Sat.
Closed Christmas, Easter and last two weeks in Aug.
● **PRICE:** Lunch €22, Dinner €34
● **CREDIT CARDS:** Visa, Mastercard

● **NOTES:**
Wheelchair access to restaurant, toilets limited access.
Children welcome, but no special menus.

● **DIRECTIONS:**
Opposite Jurys Hotel on the Western Road.

CASINO HOUSE

Kerrin & Michael Relja
Coolmain Bay, Kilbrittain,
Co Cork
Tel: (023) 49944
Fax: 49945
chouse@eircom.net

north
east
west
south

An artful and deeply considered cooking, which echoes the artful and deeply considered style of the rooms, is the Casino signature.

Michael Relja's imagination dances all around and about his cooking in the swish Casino House. Caramelised walnuts served with cream of carrot soup. Quail with a black olive and balsamic risotto. A coriander and basil pesto with lemon roasted chicken. A lavender and paprika confit with saddle of lamb. A morel-infused polenta with fillet steak. A coconut crème with pistachio and white chocolate parfait.

At every turn, Mr Relja seizes the opportunity to surprise and excite. Gifted with an unimpeachable technique, he pulls off every little cooking trick like a supremely capable culinary conjurer. It makes for cooking that is as intriguing as it is effortlessly delicious, with dinner a series of taste outposts on an imaginatively planned itinerary. Service and the rooms are splendid, and value for money is very keen indeed.

● **OPEN:** 7pm-9pm Easter-Oct, Mon-Sun, closed Wed; Nov-Dec weekends only; open Sun lunch
● **PRICE:** Lunch €22, Dinner €33, House wine €17.50
● **CREDIT CARDS:** Visa, Mastercard

● **NOTES:**
Wheelchair access. Children welcome, high chair.

● **DIRECTIONS:**
On the R600 between Timoleague and Kinsale. Signposted from Ballinspittle and from the Coolmain causeway.

THE CROSS OF CLOYNE

Colm Falvey
Cloyne,
nr Midleton,
Co Cork
Tel: (021) 465 2401
Fax: 465 2401

Modest, mighty deliciousness is Colm Falvey's signature: this cooking just oozes taste.

He is a country cook, is Colm Falvey, and his menus sing an ode to the good foods of east Cork that he celebrates in the 'Cross. Ardsallagh goat's cheese. Cuddigan's lamb. Ballycotton mackerel and prawns and monkfish. Mussels from Rossmore. Local food cooked by a local man is the foundation of his culinary philosophy, something he learnt when working with Myrtle Allen in Ballymaloe House.
But Falvey's signature style is nowadays all his own, with his fish cookery, in particular, carving an elegant arc of deliciousness with everything he cooks: fillet of cod with a smoked salmon and champ crust; prawn scampi with spicy mayonnaise; salmon with saffron potato and a lovely watercress butter sauce. He is no slouch with meat and offal, either, as a cassoulet of Cuddigan's lamb, or a salad tiede of lamb's kidneys and fresh thyme shows. You can't argue with the logic or the deliciousness of this food.

- **OPEN:** 6pm-9.30pm Wed-Sun (from 4pm Sun)
- **PRICE:** Dinner from €30, House wine €15.87
- **CREDIT CARDS:** Visa, Mastercard

- **NOTES:**
Wheelchair access (but not to toilets). Well behaved children welcome.

- **DIRECTIONS:**
Near the centre of Cloyne village, a short step or two down from the crossroads, look for the blinds.

THE CUSTOMS HOUSE

Susan Holland
& Ian Parr
The Customs House,
Baltimore,
Co Cork
Tel: (028) 20200

Unparalleled fish cookery from one of the hippest, smartest, restaurants in the country.

It's always a treat to see folk who are eating in the Custom's House for the first time.

Firstly, it takes them an eternity to make up their mind as they study the evening's dishes chalked on the blackboard by Ian Parr. They want to eat everything, you see. The duck. The turbot. The lobster. The ceviche. The black sole. The red mullet with tapenade. The brill with sauce vierge. Then they peer at the wine list, and you can see them being gob-smacked by the stonking good value of the wines on offer. Then the food arrives, and a silenced reverie falls over them as they try Sue Holland's mesmerising food. This good, this brilliant, this cheap? you can see them thinking. But, it's real, alright, The Customs House is one of the glories of Irish eating, and one of the greatest culinary adventures of your life.

● **OPEN:** 7pm-10pm Wed-Sat (open Wed-Sun high season only). Closed first week in Oct-St Patrick's Day
● **PRICE:** Dinner €23-33
● **CREDIT CARDS:** No credit cards (foreign currency accepted)

● **NOTES:**
Limited wheelchair access. Children - under 12s unlikely to feel comfortable.

● **DIRECTIONS:**
On the left hand side of the street as you enter Baltimore, beside the Garda station, 50m from the pier.

FISHY FISHY CAFÉ

Martin & Marie Shanahan
Kinsale Gourmet Store and
Fishy Fishy Café
Guardwell, Kinsale,
Co Cork
Tel: (021) 477 4453

Kinsale's got-to-be-there
destination for fab fish
cookery from Martin and
Marie and their team.

Food lovers arrive in Kinsale with one destination in mind: Martin and Marie Shanahan's brilliant Fishy Fishy Café. It's brilliant because it's logical. Mr Shanahan is up at 5am (ouch!) to source his fish, then he brings it back to Kinsale and cooks it and sells it and Marie Shanahan serves it. That's what this restaurant and fish shop is all about.

He loves to pair a sweet chilli sauce with shellfish (go for the steamed clams with chilli sauce: awesome!) and he likes to throw chickpeas into a dish whenever he gets a chance. But, for the most part, Mr Shanahan lets the flavour of the fish do the talking, so this is the simplest cooking, and if some little fillet on the wet slab takes your fancy, then he will cook that for you whatever way you fancy. Some white wine, a table out under the awning, the buzz of lovely Kinsale, and who cares that you will have to queue: this cookery is worth the wait.

- **OPEN:** 11.30am-4.30pm (shop open 9am-6pm)
- **PRICE:** Lunch €17.20, House wine €17.70
- **CREDIT CARDS:** Visa, Mastercard

- **NOTES:**
Wheelchair access, but not to toilets.
Children welcome. No smoking in restaurant.

- **DIRECTIONS:**
Next to St Multoge church, in the Guardwell section just at the north end of the town.

ISAAC'S

Canice Sharkey & Michael
& Catherine Ryan
48 MacCurtain St, Cork
Co Cork
Tel: (021) 450 3805, Fax: 455 1348
isaacs@iol.ie

Cork city's great brasserie sails on serenely, with a potent recipe for success that has largely remained unchanged over the years.

Isaac's is one of those restaurants that proves that if you get it right, then there is never a need to fix it. Fashions in food come and go, but the Isaac's formula of delicious, familiar food, served in a terrific room which enjoys a great atmosphere, with excellent value for money and shipshape service, is something none of us can ever tire of. It ain't broke, and it ain't likely to break.

Good meats from the grill, some zippy pastas and pizzas, and modern notes such as quesadillas and lively curries constitute the core of the offer. It's cooking which proudly shows its influences and its intentions: a Mediterranean-style lightness is what they aim to achieve, but, above all, Isaac's has prospered because of its striving for food that is simple and delicious: you could eat here several times a week and enjoy every experience, so welcoming and enjoyable is this food.

● **OPEN:** 12.30pm-2.30pm, 6.30pm-10.30pm Mon-Sun ('till 9pm Sun)
● **PRICE:** Lunch €10-20, Dinner €20, House wine €16
● **CREDIT CARDS:** All major cards accepted

● **NOTES:**
Full wheelchair access.
Children welcome, high chair.

● **DIRECTIONS:**
Opposite the Metropole Hotel, just north of the river.

ISLAND COTTAGE

John Desmond & Ellmary Fenton
Heir Island, Skibbereen,
Co Cork
Tel: (028) 38102, Fax: 38102
ef@islandcottage.com
http://www.islandcottage.com

There is no comparable experience to the amazing Island Cottage culinary and cultural theatre.

An evening in Heir Island is actually like a theatrical experience. The pacing of the service, the duration of the evening, the procession of food course by course, the steady and inexorable development of the theme, which is the appreciation of food at its most fundamental level, is profoundly artistic. The experience John Desmond and Ellmary Fenton create is sublime, and unforgettable.

Here is a recent dinner: chicken liver pâté on white bread, then a first course of perfect crab risotto. Sweet fillet of lamb served with benchmark gratin dauphinoise, with courgettes with wild mushrooms, and a jus of lamb juices. Gubbeen farmhouse cheese, in perfect condition. Then a delicate and refreshing green leaf salad, before a truly magnificent baked lemon soufflé that almost raised hosannas from the room. Excellent coffee, excellent wines, an experience that was perfect to the detail.

- **OPEN:** 8pm-12pm, 15 May-15 Sept. Closed Mon-Tue
- **PRICE:** Dinner €30, House wine €15
- **CREDIT CARDS:** No credit cards.

- **NOTES:**
Booking absolutely essential. Wheelchair access only with help of friends. Not recommended for children.

- **DIRECTIONS:**
The shortest ferry trip to Heir Island is from Cunnamore pier. From Skibb take the N71 to Schull. About 3 miles from Skibb there is a signpost to Heir Island. Turn left and follow the signs to Cunnamore. Drive to the very end, there is a large parking area. This is where the 4 minute ferry leaves for Heir Island.

JACOB'S ON THE MALL

Tom & Kate McCarthy
30a South Mall, Cork
Co Cork
Tel: (021) 425 1530,
Fax 425 1531
kingsley@tinet.ie

Mercy Fenton's culinary signature is forthright and fearlessly simple.

Mercy Fenton could act as an archetype for the way in which women's cooking differs from men's. She works with her ingredients in a way which is subtle, persuasive and satisfying, but avoids the transformatory bravado which is the hallmark of the way in which male chefs work with food.

Instead, the food in Jacob's is more about sourcing and showcasing: grilled oysters with shallots, garlic and tarragon butter; rump of venison with celeriac and parsnip purée; duck with spiced sweet potatoes and ginger jus; summer fruit trifle with mascarpone. Here, impeccable ingredients are matched with the most suitable partners: Ms Fenton acts almost as a matchmaker, which means Jacob's is some sort of culinary dating agency – and the result: happy families all round, that's for sure. A fabulous restaurant.

● **OPEN:** 12.30pm-2.30pm, 6.30pm-10pm Mon-Sat
● **PRICE:** Lunch €23, Dinner €35,
House wine €16.50
● **CREDIT CARDS:** Visa, Mastercard, Amex

● **NOTES:**
Full wheelchair access. Children welcome.
Happy to cater for vegans and other dietary requirements.

● **DIRECTIONS:**
A south city centre restaurant, at the Grand Parade end of South Mall, next to the bank.

JACQUES

**Jacqueline Barry &
Eithne Barry
Phoenix Street,
Cork,
Tel: (021) 427 7387
Fax: 427 0634**

**Want to feel twenty years
younger? Dinner in
Jacques should do the trick.**

What is the secret of eternal youth? We don't know,
unfortunately, but we have a sneaking suspicion that Jacq
and Eithne Barry, owners of Jacques Restaurant, know
exactly what it is.

How else can you explain how they play such truly funky
music (one of the best soundtracks you can hear), cook
such truly funky food, and serve it with such sassy style.
Of course, other people do that also, but Jacq and Eithne
have been doing it this well for more than twenty years,
now. Eternal youth. Nothing else can explain it.

Recently, we had simple, soulful plaice in a beer batter
with pea purée, and cracking chicken Bengal with rice and
pickles. There was a lovely antipasti of English Market
charcuterie, fine roasted aubergine and peppers with
Ardsallagh cheese, perfect crème brulée and bread and
butter pud, gorgeous wines. All in all a sublime slice of
youthful energy.

● **OPEN:** Noon-3pm Mon-Fri, 6pm-10pm Tue-Sat
● **PRICE:** Lunch from €15.10, Dinner €31.60, House
wine €11.90
● **CREDIT CARDS:** Visa, Mastercard, Amex

● **NOTES:**
Early dinner, two course, 6pm-7pm Mon-Sat.
No wheelchair access.
Children welcome to 7.30pm

● **DIRECTIONS:**
Just behind the GPO in the centre of Cork.

LONGUEVILLE HOUSE

The O'Callaghan family
The President's Restaurant,
Mallow, Co Cork
Tel: (022) 47156, Fax: 47459
info@longuevillehouse.ie
www.longuevillehouse.ie

No one else cooks like William O'Callaghan, a chef of the most amazing ability and imagination.

"Well cultured mastery" was the phrase some friends came up with to attempt to describe the sheer brilliance of William O'Callaghan's cooking.

It's a good phrase too, for mastery of the culture of cooking in all its forms and complexities is what Mr O'Callaghan demonstrates. He is - perhaps more than almost anyone else in Ireland - a total cook. He understands his ingredients implicitly, understands his technique intimately, understands the choreographies of taste and texture down to his fingertips.

The results of this deep culture are fabulous: superlative pâtés and terrines made with Longueville pork; Blackwater salmon smoked in house and served with gribiche sauce; sea bass with a scallop and lemon balm mousse; Longueville lamb in a potato and herb crust, outstanding desserts. Service is as inspired as the food.

- **OPEN:** 7pm-9pm Mon-Sun
- **PRICE:** Dinner €47-61
- **CREDIT CARDS:** All major cards accepted.

- **NOTES:**
Recommended for vegetarians and vegans. Conference centre, takes 45. Private dining room. Wheelchair access through courtyard. Children welcome.

- **DIRECTIONS:**
3 miles west of Mallow on the N72 to Killarney. Take Ballyclough junction to the right and hotel entrance is 100 yards on left side.

10 RESTAURANTS
WITH GREAT VALUE

1

ALDEN'S
BELFAST, NORTHERN IRELAND

2

KEVIN ARUNDEL @ NUMBER 10
DUBLIN, CO DUBLIN

3

THE CUSTOMS HOUSE
BALTIMORE, CO CORK

4

DUKE'S RESTAURANT
WARRENPOINT, NORTHERN IRELAND

5

LA MARINE
ROSSLARE, CO WEXFORD

6

THE NUREMORE HOTEL
CARRICKMACROSS, CO MONAGHAN

7

O'CONNELL'S
DUBLIN, CO DUBLIN

8

101 TALBOT
DUBLIN, CO DUBLIN

9

PACKIE'S
KENMARE, CO KERRY

10

ZUNI
KILKENNY, CO KILKENNY

O'CALLAGHAN-WALSHE

Sean Kearney
The Square, Rosscarbery,
West Cork
Tel: (023) 48125,
Fax: 48125
funfish@indigo.ie

One of the great West Cork icon addresses, in one of the country's great rooms.

Roxanne Kearney (aged 5) helps to make the scampi in O'C-W, and this girl is going to shape up into some cook, because she is learning in one of the country's best restaurants.

Everyone loves O'C-W. What's to love? The room for a start, which looks more like a stage set of a restaurant than a real restaurant. The service by Sean Kearney, which is amusing, amused, terrific. And Martina O'Donovan's cooking, which is truly the business: spicy fishcakes with chermoulah to begin, maybe the hot prawns with lemon and garlic. Then some scallops with basil crème fraîche, or john dory with a cider and mussel sauce. But hey, let's encourage youthful endeavour, and choose Roxanne's Homemade Prawn Scampi. Don't miss the rainwater syllabub, and don't miss the fantastic Trinity burnt cream. Only brilliant.

● **OPEN:** For Dinner only. Weekends only in Winter. Full time from May to Oct.
● **PRICE:** Dinner €34, House Wine €17.70, or €4.40 a glass (from a choice of six).
● **CREDIT CARDS:** Visa, Mastercard

● **NOTES:**
Limited Wheelchair Access. Children welcome 'if friendly and unarmed'.

● **DIRECTIONS:**
Rosscarbery is approached on the N71. The restaurant is on the northern side of the main square.

OTTO'S CREATIVE CUISINE

Hilda & Otto Kunze
Dunworley, Butlerstown,
Bandon, Co Cork
Tel: (023) 40461
ottokunze@eircom.net
www. ottoscreativecatering.com

Holistic, spiritual cooking
from one of the great masters
of contemporary Irish
cookery.

Teacher. Grower. Chef. Farmer. Thinker. Pioneer.
Otto Kunze is the renaissance man writ large, a powerful
and practical advocate for good food, real food, good
cooking, real cooking.
You will find tastes and textures in OCC which can't be
found or enjoyed anywhere else. The sheer quality of the
raw ingredients with which Mr Kunze cooks is beyond
compare: the freshest fish, well-minded pork; superb beef,
annotated with wild and organically grown ingredients
that sing with flavour: Ummera smoked eel and salmon
on organic leaves; bacon and cabbage soup made with
Shetland kale and Ummera bacon; salmon and monkfish
on sea spinach; salad with warm roasted pheasant; braised
ox-tongue with port wine sauce; roast organic lamb with
its own gravy; superb apple strudel with lush, rich ice
cream. Food for the soul, no less.

● **OPEN:** 7pm-9.30pm, Sun lunch
● **PRICE:** Lunch €25, Dinner €40
● **CREDIT CARDS:** Visa, Mastercard

● **NOTES:**
Reservations only. Bring your own wine, no corkage.
Wheelchair access to dining room.
Children welcome.

● **DIRECTIONS:**
From Bandon go to Timoleague, follow signs to
Barryroe until you come across signs to Dunworley. The
entrance is marked OCC Restaurant and B&B.

THE CORNCRAKE

**Brid McCartney &
Noreen Lynch
The Corncrake,
Carndonagh,
Co Donegal
Tel: (077) 74534**

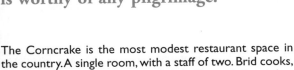

It's a long, long way up north, but The Corncrake is worthy of any pilgrimage.

The Corncrake is the most modest restaurant space in the country. A single room, with a staff of two. Brid cooks, Noreen does all the other bits and pieces, and together they run one of the best-loved restaurants.

So, what's to love? Well, aside from the maternal service, there are a series of dishes that effortlessly achieve benchmark status. The crab vinaigrette. The mature cheddar and chive soufflé. The nettle and fresh herb soup. The duck confit with hoisin. The chicken with tarragon butter. The rack of lamb with Puy lentils. The wild salmon with foaming hollandaise. Tasty food, as the pros say.

If the savoury cooking is benchmark, the sweet baking is stratospheric, especially the rhubarb ice cream and their trademark orange pannacotta. You would happily pay mighty money for this sort of cooking, but it's almost impossible to dole out any more than €25 per head.

- **OPEN:** 6pm-10pm Mon-Sun. Weekends only Oct-Jun
- **PRICE:** Dinner €25, House wine €13
- **CREDIT CARDS:** No credit cards

- **NOTES:**
Sterling cheques accepted. No wheelchair access.
Children welcome early evening only.

- **DIRECTIONS:**
Just a few minutes from the Diamond in Carndonagh.
Note: The Corncrake is moving premises to another town centre location in Spring 2002. Telephone for details.

THE FLEET INN

Marguerite Howley
Killybegs, Co Donegal
Tel: (073) 31518,
Fax: 31664
fleetinn@irishmarine.com
www.irishmarine.com/fleetinn

Delicious fish cookery, great sounds, great service, good value.
Has to be The Fleet in Killybegs then, doesn't it?

Marguerite Howley and her female team have the energy, and it shows in both the food and service in their up-above-the-pub restaurant in the centre of Killybegs.

There is a generosity of spirit about this place which is truly gratifying, a young team enjoying their work, and getting a kick out of customers who are getting a kick out of such good cooking.

And good cooking is what the Fleet Inn sends forth. Toothy crab with guacamole and tomato confit; prawns — wisely cooked in their shells for maximum flavour — and tossed in garlic butter; blackened mackerel with sweet salsa; perfect turbot with a lime and dill butter sauce; and for those crazy enough not to choose fish there is always good local lamb and beef, cooked with respect.

The staff are only brilliant, and so is the music — these girls really like their grooves — and value is excellent.

● **OPEN:** 7pm-10pm Mon-Sun (Tue-Sat off season, closed 17 Feb-17 Mar)
● **PRICE:** Dinner €27-30
● **CREDIT CARDS:** Visa, Mastercard, Laser

● **NOTES:**
No wheelchair access.
Children, no facilities.
Reservations recommended, especially in high season.

● **DIRECTIONS:**
In the centre of Killybegs.

KEALY'S SEAFOOD BAR

James & Tricia Kealy
Greencastle,
Co Donegal
Tel: (077) 81010, Fax: 81010
kealys@iol.ie

Every coastal town needs a Kealy's, but Greencastle wisely shows no sign of letting its favourite fish restaurant move anywhere.

Don't let the simple appearance of Kealy's lead you into thinking that it's any sort of run-of-the-mill place. This is one of the key destination addresses for fine fish cookery in Ireland, a place where James and Tricia Kealy demonstrate professionalism and consistency, and a passionate understanding for good cooking.

Their success is explained by the fact that they really look after their customers. You should come here to eat fish and shellfish, of course, but if you feel like meat, they cook fine meat, and vegetarians are well looked after with creative, imaginative dishes. But the classical and smart fish cookery is terrific: oysters Pearl of the Foyle – a gratin of oysters and smoked salmon served on toasted croûtes – john dory with an anchovy butter; turbot with Stilton; smoked haddock florentine. Book in advance for weekends: it gets seriously packed.

● **OPEN:** 12.30pm-5pm bar snacks, 7pm-9.30pm Tue-Sun (closed Mon-Wed off season)
● **PRICE:** Snacks €3-10, Dinner €30,
House wine €11
● **CREDIT CARDS:** Visa, Mastercard, Amex

● **NOTES:**
Wheelchair access.
Children welcome lunch and early evening, high chair.

● **DIRECTIONS:**
On the seafront in Greencastle, opposite the harbour.

THE MILL RESTAURANT

Derek & Susan Alcorn
Figart, Dunfanaghy, Letterkenny,
Co Donegal
Tel/Fax: (074) 36985
themillrestaurant@oceanfree.net
www.themillrestaurant.com

Beautiful cooking from Derek Alcorn has made The Mill the hot spot in the north west with locals and holidaymakers.

There is a lovely simplicity and directness to Derek Alcorn's cooking, a trueness of aim that explains how The Mill has become such a destination address in a relatively short space of time.

He never pushes the boat too far out into wild waters, nor does he err on the side of caution. Instead he is looking always for the best pairings for his main ingredients: lobster ragoût with Sheephaven Bay salmon; grated spuds and pancetta with fillet steak; Doe Castle mussels with Smithwicks and sage; lime and coriander couscous with mushroom and aubergine moussaka; fried anchovies with seabass salad; rhubarb and white chocolate trifle; chocolate fondant with pistachio ice cream. This is neat, wise cooking, and the service and presentation of the food is just as sharp, just as disarming. Do book one of the stylish rooms and stay over.

- **OPEN:** 7pm-9pm Tue-Sun, 12.30pm-2pm Sun
- **PRICE:** Lunch €5, Dinner €44, House wine €19
- **CREDIT CARDS:** Visa, Mastercard, Electron

- **NOTES:**
Wheelchair access to restaurant only. Children welcome.

- **DIRECTIONS:**
Half mile past the village of Dunfanaghy, beside the lake. 30 miles from Carrickfinn airport, 60 miles from Eglinton Airport, 27 miles from Letterkenny, 140 miles from Belfast.

AQUA RESTAURANT

Richard Clery & Charlie Smith
1 West Pier, Howth, Co Dublin
Tel: (01) 832 0690 Fax: 832 0687
dine@aqua.ie
www.aqua.ie

Brian Daly's classic, elegant and welcoming cooking has seen Aqua rise above all the local competition in Howth.

Aqua hangs literally over the water at the end of Howth pier, but if the views over to Ireland's Eye are serene, this former yacht club's history has been less smooth. But now, with Brian Daly at the stoves and Charlie Smith masterminding the room, Aqua has found its groove, and is producing impressive, confident modern Irish cooking. As you would expect of a former Cooke's Café chef, classic dishes are done just right: their Caesar salad is fabulous, skewered tiger prawns with chilli and aioli are teasingly tasty, a main course of scallops with mango and chilli salsa is executed to perfection; grilled salmon is kept simple and is very pleasing. The dry-aged sirloin with grilled peppers and roasted baby potatoes is just the sort of smart, consistent cooking that is Aqua's trademark. A walk followed by a drink in the bar and a Sunday lunch will convince you of the merits of the bourgeois life.

- **OPEN:** bar lunch 1pm-3.30pm, 5.30pm-11pm Tue-Sat, Sun brunch 12.30pm-6pm
- **PRICE:** Bar lunch €8, Lunch €24, Dinner €35, House wine €14
- **CREDIT CARDS:** All major cards accepted

- **NOTES:**
No wheelchair access. Children welcome.

- **DIRECTIONS:**
On west pier in Howth, from the DART station, turn left and follow to the end of the pier (five minute walk).

BANG CAFÉ

Chris & Simon Stokes
11 Merrion Row,
Dublin 2
Tel: (01) 676 0898, Fax: 676 0899
www.bangrestaurant.com

Bang is making a big noise right now. A second branch will surely be called The Boom Boom Room, right?

Bang is right. Bang on target with the food, with the service, and bang on target with a hip crowd who enjoy this svelte space. Chef Lorcan Gribbin and his team offer the sort of eclectic menu that threatens too much from too many places, but the reality is that Bang offers sharp cooking, such as excellent salad leaves with shrimp spring rolls, or delicate-as-eyelashes baby spinach leaves served with plum tomatoes and crispy prosciuttio (memo to Irish kitchens; fellas, can we lose the crispy Serranos, Parmas and prosciuttios, please. Enough already).

Even better are the mains; roast brill is cooked to perfection, with ace shallots and salsify. Chicken chasseur is fab: crisp pieces of chicken from wing and thigh with great mushroom and red winey sauce. Food this good has found its audience quickly, and smart guys choose the seats as the banquette in the dining room is too low.

● **OPEN:** 12.30pm-3pm Mon-Sat, 6pm-10.30pm Mon-Wed, 6pm-11pm Thu-Sat
● **PRICE:** Lunch €18-25, Dinner €35-40, House wine €17.70
● **CREDIT CARDS:** All major cards accepted

● **NOTES:**
No wheelchair access. Children welcome.

● **DIRECTIONS:**
From the top of Grafton Street, turn left, walk parallel to St Stephen's Green for about 5 minutes. The restaurant is just beyond the end of the Green, beside the Bank of Ireland cash machine.

BOND

Karl M. Purdy
5 Beresford Place, Dublin 1
Tel: (01) 855 9244 Fax: 888 1612
info@bond.ie
www.BOND.ie

Karl Purdy and his team know what people want: great room, great food, great wines at great value. Simple, really.

A one-of-a-kind on the Dublin restaurant scene, this one-year-old up-and-comer is blessed with loads of natural talent, energy and verve. Head chef Ross Zolynsky, sommelier Julien le Gentil and owner Karl Purdy demonstrate an easy confidence and personal style, and it seems to attract an adventurous, eclectic lot; everyone from business people to arty types (and anyone else) enjoy lunch, dinner or just a bottle of wine in Bond. The cooking is sophisticated-rustic, and the kitchen is not afraid to use a specific seasonal ingredient — pears, shiitakes, or Gorgonzola cheese, for example — in different dishes on the same menu. Vegetables are a strong point, as in a pasta dish with snow peas, pesto and sun-dried tomatoes or rack of lamb with an earthy fennel and root vegetable gratin, garnished with a huge roasted shiitake and star anise. A true hot spot, real hot.

- **OPEN:** noon-3pm Mon-Fri, 6pm-9pm Mon-Wed, 6pm-10pm Sat. Closed Sun.
- **PRICE:** Dinner €35. All wine sold at retail price plus €6.35
- **CREDIT CARDS:** Visa, Mastercard, Laser

- **NOTES:**
Children, no special facilities. No wheelchair access. Personalised wine tasting for groups of 6-12. Wine shop opening soon.

- **DIRECTIONS:**
At the very bottom of Lower Gardiner Street, facing the Customs House, around the corner from Busarus.

BRUNO'S

Bruno Berta
21 Kildare Street, Dublin 2
Tel: (01) 662 4724,
Fax: 662 3857
www.brunos.ie

Knockout savoury cooking from young Garret Byrne, but the sweet cooking has some way to go to match the savoury stuff.

The basement Bruno's used to be a restaurant where civil servants from the Dept. of Agriculture and ladies of a certain class and age went to eat lunch. Raymond Blanc once asked a waitress in here what the stuffed pork was stuffed with. "Stuffing," she replied.

Now, it is Bruno Berta's second Dublin city restaurant. Young Garrett Byrne, a graduate of the Nico's academy, has charge of the stoves, the waitresses are hip and funky and the savoury cooking is only ace. A boudin of crab with crushed broad beans and velouté of basil is pitch-perfect bistro food, pot roasted guinea fowl with pea purée and a pancetta and cep risotto is even better, and Mr Byrne's fish cookery is just as precise: roast sea bass with ratatouille, saffron potatoes and caponata is excellent. Desserts, however, can be dire, and need work, but, otherwise, Bruno's Kildare Street is a hot spot.

● **OPEN:** Noon-2.30pm Mon-Fri, 6pm-10.30pm Mon-Sat
● **PRICE:** Lunch from €18.50, Dinner €30-40, House wine €19
● **CREDIT CARDS:** All major cards accepted

● **NOTES:**
No wheelchair access. Children welcome, no facilities.

● **DIRECTIONS:**
Just off St Stephen's Green, opposite Leinster House, down the road from Shelburne Hotel, in the basement of Mitchell's wine store.

CAVISTON'S

The Caviston family
59 Glasthule Road, Sandycove
Dun Laoghaire, Co Dublin
Tel: (01) 280 9245, Fax: 284 4054
caviston@indigo.ie
www.cavistons.com

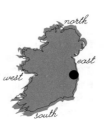

The busiest lunchtime restaurant on the planet, and one of the best-loved restaurants in Ireland.

In Caviston's they do not one, not two, but three services of lunch. A speedy 90 minutes from noon, then turn the tables for the next hour and a half, before the final sitting kicks in at 3pm. Six days a week equals 18 lunch services, and 18 squadrons of happy fish lovers who bless the day the Caviston brothers decided to start cooking the fish the family shop had been selling for decades.

Noel Cusack mans the stoves, and the secret of their unbelievable success lies in cooking the freshest fish they can get: at 10.30am some days there won't even be a menu written. Then, suddenly, it's pell-mell crazy as the dishes are invented and prepped: crab claws in tempura batter; fresh haddock with toothy tartare; lobster with garlic and herb butter; their trademark seafood pie; chargrilled swordfish with mojo picon; salad of Boston shrimps. The cooking leaves no argument, save for what to drink with this lovely seafood.

● **OPEN:** three lunch sittings per day: noon-1.30pm, 1.30pm-3pm, 3pm-close Tue-Fri; noon-1.45pm, 1.45pm-3.15pm, 3.15pm-close Sat
● **PRICE:** Lunch €20-30,
House wine €16.50
● **CREDIT CARDS:** All major cards accepted

● **NOTES:**
No wheelchair access. Reservations essential. Children welcome, high chair.

● **DIRECTIONS:**
In the centre of the village, beside Caviston's Deli.

CHAPTER ONE

Ross Lewis & Martin Corbett
18/19 Parnell Square, Dublin 1
Tel: (01) 873 2266,
Fax: 873 2330
info@chapteronerestaurant.com
www.chapteronerestaurant.com

Sublime, mature cooking
from Ross Lewis and his
team is the real theatre in
this neck of the woods.

Ross Lewis and Martin Corbett were true pioneers when they opened in Parnell Square just over a decade ago. Tough enough opening a serious restaurant back then, but doing so on the northside must have seemed mad. But they have persevered, and they have prospered, and they have done so because they are bloody good at what they do. Cooking and service here have a mature fluency and confidence that comes from sheer hard work and constant study, with the result that Chapter One has as powerful a signature as any Dublin restaurant.

The food is, well, the food is just pure delicious: jellied ham with organic egg and parsley purée; hot oysters with spinach, bacon and bearnaise; woodcock with swede and savoy cabbage; monkfish with colcannon, modern Irish cooking with superb organic ingredients. Don't miss their pre- and post- theatre treats, when you can have two courses before and dessert after.

- **OPEN:** 12.30pm-2.30pm Tue-Fri, 6pm-11pm Tue-Sat
- **PRICE:** Lunch €27.50, Dinner €42
- **CREDIT CARDS:** Visa, Mastercard, Amex, Diners

- **NOTES:**
No wheelchair access.
Children, no facilities.

- **DIRECTIONS:**
Go left around the Rotunda Hospital at the end of O'Connell Street. Then continue, right, around Parnell Sq, and the restaurant is located just before Findlater's Church, and beside the Hugh Lane Gallery.

10 RESTAURANTS
FOR GREAT ROMANCE

1
BROCKA-ON-THE WATER
KILGARVAN QUAY, CO TIPP

2
AN CARN
RING, CO WATERFORD

3
CAYENNE
BELFAST, NORTHERN IRELAND

4
BALLYMALOE HOUSE
SHANAGARRY, CO CORK

5
THE CHART HOUSE
DINGLE, CO KERRY

6
JACOB'S LADDER
DUBLIN, CO DUBLIN

7
NIMMO'S
GALWAY, CO GALWAY

8
THE STRAWBERRY TREE
MACREDDIN, CO WICKLOW

9
THE TEA ROOM
DUBLIN, CO DUBLIN

10
ZUNI
KILKENNY, CO KILKENNY

THE COMMONS

Mike Fitzgerald
Newman House,
85-86 St Stephen's Green, D2
Tel: (01) 478 0530 Fax: 478 0551
sales@thecommonsrestaurant.ie
www.thecommonsrestaurant.ie

Aiden Byrne is the hottest
young talent in the city,
beyond argument. Queue up
to be amazed.

A food writer friend once praised Aiden Byrne's cooking,
in The Commons Restaurant, as enjoying "the poetry of
the instant".
If that is the sort of phrase that gives food writing a bad
name, it is the sort of hyperbole food writing has to reach
towards to try to capture what this young cook does. For
Aiden Byrne is pushing the culinary envelope with his
cooking, and it's a pure thrill.
He likes the sort of foodie games that have become
fashionable - red mullet three ways; assiette of foie gras;
even entire menus based around a single ingredient - but
there is no grandstanding in his food. This is a man who
squeezes out flavour, whatever he is handling, and his food
is darling, rather than fussy: cannelloni of sweetbreads
with truffle jus; salt cod brandade with fennel soup; pot
roast veal cutlet with fresh girolles and baby parsnips. Just
don't miss this... poetry of the instant.

● **OPEN:** 12.30pm-2.15pm Mon-Fri, 7pm-10.30pm
Mon-Sat
● **PRICE:** Dinner €73, House wine €22
● **CREDIT CARDS:** Visa, Mastercard, Amex

● **NOTES:**
Wheelchairs — restaurant located in basement, help
needed on stairs, otherwise all on level ground.
No facilities for children.

● **DIRECTIONS:**
Beside the University church on the south side of St
Stephen's Green, in the centre of Dublin.

COOKE'S CAFÉ

John Cooke
14 Sth William Street,
Dublin 2
Tel: (01) 679 0536 Fax: 679 0546
cookes1@iol.ie
www.cookescafe.com

A new decade for Cooke's will see a major transformation towards a more informal, accessible style of dining, and a new name.

John Cooke has always been as adept a student of the Dublin restaurant business as he has been one of the city's leading chefs. Now, after a decade of success as Cooke's Café, he is planning a radical transformation of this Dublin destination, creating two floors for eating and drinking where the style will be relaxed, informal, without any manner of structure. If you simply want a glass of wine and to graze on some food, tapas-style, then you can head upstairs. Downstairs, open plan kitchens, a wood-burning stove and a very limited bookings policy will see a more laid-back ambience, in tune with the way we all want to eat now. There will be a more modest mark-up on the wines also, all aiming to allow one to eat here for moderate cost, but in the same swish and stylish style that has been a hallmark of Cooke's. Frankly, we can't wait for mid-summer.

- **OPEN:** 11am-11pm Mon-Sun
- **PRICE:** Meals €10-30
- **CREDIT CARDS:** All major cards accepted

- **NOTES:**
Wheelchair access to ground floor only, but not to toilets.
Children welcome if well behaved.

- **DIRECTIONS:**
Opposite the rere entrance to the Powerscourt Town House Centre, on a road parallel to Grafton Street.

DISH

**Trevor Browne &
Gerard Foote
146 Upper Leeson St,
Dublin 4
Tel: (01) 664 2135
Fax: 664 2136**

Rebirthed on the southside, Dish is one of the quintessential modern Dublin city restaurants, hip, savvy and fun.

Trevor Browne and Gerard Foote are fast becoming the Chris Corbin and Jeremy King of Dublin, restaurateurs who know exactly how to make a restaurant concept work. They have relocated Dish from its Temple Bar abode to a much more suitable space on the corner of smart Leeson Street, close to their other sure-fire success, Tribeca, which is on the strip of Ranelagh.
Dish enjoys a lovely series of rooms, and lovely food, all served with capacious ease and charm. Confit of bacon with white beans, garlic and parsley is clever trencherman food; coconut and ginger crêpes with shredded duck and hoisin typical of their Asian flights of fancy. Crispy fried skate with ginger vinaigrette is perfect; butternut squash risotto wholesome and light, whilst spiced lamb kebabs are spot on. The cheese board is sourced from Sheridan's Cheesemongers and is one of the finest in the city.

● **OPEN:** noon-4pm, 6pm-11pm Mon-Sun
● **PRICE:** Lunch €20-25, Dinner €35-40, House wine €17.50
● **CREDIT CARDS:** All major cards accepted

● **NOTES:**
No wheelchair access, though more than happy to help.
Children welcome.
Reservations necessary.

● **DIRECTIONS:**
Near the Burlington Hotel, across the road from O'Briens pub.

L'ECRIVAIN

**Derry & Sally Anne Clarke
109 Lower Baggot Street,
Dublin 2
Tel: (01) 661 1919, Fax: 661 0617
enquiries@lecrivain.com
www.lecrivain.com**

The real pleasure of Dublin dining is found – at its zenith – in Derry Clarke's brilliant L'Ecrivain.

L'Ecrivain is as good as, if not better than, it has ever been. Derry and Sally-Anne Clarke are equally adept at making their restaurant clubby and au fait for suits and socialites, and intimate and atmospheric for the evening crowd. Mr Clarke elevates a simple menu to incredible heights: sweet Dublin Bay prawns in ketaifi pastry with a plummy chilli jam kick-starts the appetite; gamey pan-seared wood pigeon breast with caramelised shiitakes is garnished with a jaunty rasher, a plume of chive and silky truffle cream. Masculine rump of lamb is gussied up with a slab of buttery foie gras and garnishes of mustardy caper mash and citricised pepper glaze. White and dark chocolate parfait is sandwiched between chocolate cardamom biscuits. You can't do better than Derry Clarke's totally personal, passionate yet balanced cuisine. He truly makes people understand the real pleasure of dining.

- **OPEN:** 12.30pm-2pm Mon-Fri, 7pm-11pm Mon-Sat
- **PRICE:** Lunch €27-31.50, Dinner €50, House wine €25
- **CREDIT CARDS:** All major cards accepted

- **NOTES:**
Wheelchair access on ground floor.
Children welcome if well behaved. Service charge only on food.

- **DIRECTIONS:**
Through the archway, beside Lad Lane. Across the road from the Bank of Ireland on Baggot Street.

ELEPHANT & CASTLE

George Schwarz
18-19 Temple Bar,
Dublin 2
Tel: (01) 679 3121,
Fax: 679 1956
ecdublin@eircom.net

The great Temple Bar stalwart has a new team, but consistency and imagination remain, and it's as difficult as ever to get a seat.

Many people reckoned that without Liz Mee and John Hayes – who powerhoused the E&C to the status of a Dublin institution since the restaurant opened in 1989 – that the Elephant could not survive. But survive it has, maintaining an impressive consistency and delivery under head chef Mark Wilkins which has seen the old trooper hold onto its devotees, who have to wait just as long as ever to get a table here in the evening.

The formula remains much the same as ever: the omelettes, the chicken wings, the daily specials, the excellent burgers, the good weekend brunch which remains a staple of city life. The sounds are cool, the staff carefully trained, the drinks and coffees good. It has been quite a major achievement to keep the E&C just as sharp and as up-to-the-minute as it has always been.

● **OPEN:** 8am-11.30pm Mon-Fri, 10.30am-11.30pm Sat, noon-11.30pm Sun
● **PRICE:** Lunch €10, Dinner €30, House wine €18.40
● **CREDIT CARDS:** Visa, Mastercard, Amex, Diners

● **NOTES:**
Wheelchairs: ground floor access, no wheelchair toilet. Children welcome.

● **DIRECTIONS:**
In the centre of Dublin, in the heart of Temple Bar, just off Temple Bar Square, just south of the River Liffey.

HALO

The Morrison Hotel
Ormond Quay, Dublin 1
Tel: (01) 887 2421, Fax: 878 3185
halo@morrisonhotel.ie
www.morrisonhotel.ie

Coolest room, coolest
sounds, and oh so hip.
Don't miss the desserts.

Everyone in the room is wearing black, the sounds conjure industrial-era Stina Nordenstam to show just how hip they are, and if you weren't confident then Halo would almost be too, too much to bear.

But, ignore the fashion following, start eating, and right from the superb white bread rolls through to the incredible desserts, you will see why Halo survives and thrives; the food is ace. That cappuccino of Dublin Bay prawns is intense, but never heavy, and its simplicity is winning; the braised scallion with roast sea bass is just the right note to match a yam mash, and the desserts are just to die for: probably the best in town, so save space for thrills such as Valrhona caraibe chocolate and lime mousse with a winter fruit compote, which dances with sprayed plates, gold leaf and the exuberance of great art. Good staff, who really enjoy serving children.

- **OPEN:** 7.30am-10.30am, 12.30pm-2.30pm, 7pm-10.30pm Mon-Sun
- **PRICE:** Lunch €24-26, Dinner €45-60, House wine €20.95
- **CREDIT CARDS:** All major cards accepted.

- **NOTES:**
Full wheelchair access. Street parking, and nearby carparks. Children welcome.

- **DIRECTIONS:**
In the centre of the city, opposite the new Millennium Bridge on Ormond Quay.

JACOB'S LADDER

Adrian & Bernie Roche
4-5 Nassau Street, Dublin 2
Tel: (01) 670 3865
Fax: 670 3868
www.jacobsladder.ie

One of the real cult Dublin addresses, with some of the most knowing and imaginative food you can enjoy.

A chef who is modest and shy virtually to the point of invisibility, Adrian Roche enjoys one vital asset: his cooking doesn't merely speak for him, it broadcasts for him that here is a cook with true skill, originality and signature style, one of the most impressive talents at work in the capital.

Like the man, the cooking is subtle, unforced, but wonderfully connected: terrine of game birds with fried apple and blueberries is the sort of skilled game with techniques and flavours he loves, and that skill means that even complex sounding mains, such as sea bass with ratatouille, fennel purée, spinach, garlic mash and a saffron and orange sauce, is magisterially controlled and executed, with not a superfluous gesture. Ambition and execution marry well here, with not a weak offering on a large menu. Service is great, the room relaxed and lovely.

● **OPEN:** 12.30pm-2.30pm, 6pm-10.30pm Tue-Sat
● **PRICE:** Lunch €23, Dinner €43,
House wine €18.50
● **CREDIT CARDS:** All major cards accepted

● **NOTES:**
No wheelchair access.
Children welcome.

● **DIRECTIONS:**
Upstairs, over the vegetable shop, overlooking Trinity College, close to the Kilkenny Design shop.

KEVIN ARUNDEL @ No 10

Kevin Arundel
10 Lower Fitzwilliam St,
Dublin 2
Tel: (01) 676 1060 Fax: 676 1542
info@longfields.ie
www.kevinarundel.com

Excellent, modest cooking and a happening team of youngsters are making waves in Kevin Arundel's Number 10.

He is a good cook, Kevin Arundel, and he has succeeded in making a success out of the basement dining room of Number 10. Arundel had a spell with Derry Clarke in L'Ecrivain before opening, and it shows in a new confidence with flavours: hot Carlingford oysters with mango curry and sabayon is a tribute to a L'Ecrivain speciality, but it's a gee-whizz of a dish in its own right, a great starter. A velouté of spiced mussels with slender pasta noodles is beautifully achieved. Roasted sea bass — now that it is farmed, this once rare fish is suddenly everywhere — with chorizo and tapenade and sauce vierge is just right, a lovely lesson in contrasting flavours and textures. They serve a fine cheeseboard, and sweet, simple desserts such as a winter berry soufflé are a treat. Above all, Number 10 works thanks to a talented and committed young team who really enjoy their work.

- **OPEN:** noon-2.30pm, 7pm-10.30pm Mon-Sun (closed 10pm Sun)
- **PRICE:** Lunch €20-24, Dinner €40, House wine €20
- **CREDIT CARDS:** All major cards accepted.

- **NOTES:**
Private dining in Georgian Dublin setting. Wheelchair access. Children welcome.

- **DIRECTIONS:**
Larry Murphy's pub off Baggot Street is the nearest landmark. Road runs between Merrion Sq and Baggot Street, beside the ESB headquarters.

KISH RESTAURANT

Cathy Delaney
Coliemore Road, Dalkey
Co Dublin
Tel: (01) 285 0377
Fax: 285 0141
book@kishrestaurant.ie

Don't let the bourgeois setting put you off: Kish is a warmly welcoming restaurant with some really smart seafood cookery.

Kish is a serious seafood restaurant in a seriously beautiful setting, but it's also warm. From manageress Michelle Delaney, whose family built the 60-seat eatery in 2000, to the attentive wait staff, there's an obligingness that defies the condescension peculiar to some top restaurants.

Newly arrived chef Sean Murphy (late of Paul Rankin in Belfast, and Nico Ladenis and Gordon Ramsay in London) works in a French tradition. His cooking is technically brilliant but expressive: ravioli of salmon and langoustine, covered with oyster cappuccino, tastes like the sea and looks like a pulsing sea creature alive with delicacy; perfectly roasted escalope of salmon arrives in a bilious-looking orange sweet and sour pepper sauce that's as smooth, deep and rich as velvet. Wines are overpriced, Sunday lunch is a great deal, and here is a radical, real new arrival.

- **OPEN:** 12.30pm-2pm Thur-Sun, 7pm-10pm Wed-Sun
- **PRICE:** Lunch €20-30, Dinner €35, House wine €20
- **CREDIT CARDS:** Visa, Mastercard, Amex, Diners

● **NOTES:**
Full wheelchair access. Children - no facilities. Reservations essential. Private parties and small weddings (max 60) catered for.

● **DIRECTIONS:**
8 miles south of Dublin city centre, on the coast road, facing Dalkey Island, on the south end of Dalkey.

THE MERMAID CAFÉ

Ben Gorman & Mark Harrell
69/70 Dame Street,
Temple Bar, Dublin 2
Tel: (01) 670 8236, Fax: 670 8205
mermaid@iol.ie
www.mermaid.ie

You really should take a first-timer to the Mermaid, just to see them go doolalley delighted.

There are folk out there – lots of 'em – who are Mermaid zealots. "Have you tried the smoked haddock! – the antipasti! – the crab cakes! – the pheasant! – the spicy pecans! – the sea bass! – the pecan tart! – the malted ice cream!" Yeah, you say, aren't they great? "Great! Great!? They are awesome, awesome," and off they go, zealots for the cause of the lovely Mermaid. The Mermaid deserves such good people proselytising on its behalf. Its food is distinctive, delicious and free of any clichés. They really do make it up on the spot in here, save for a few staples like the crab cakes that they just can't take off the menu, and vital things such as service, the music they play, the design of the room, and the wine list are done with just as much creativity and imagination as you will find in the cooking. There is nowhere else like it, so go on: be a Mermaid zealot: proselytise.

● **OPEN:** 12.30pm-2.30pm, 6pm-11pm Mon-Sat, 12.30pm-3.30pm Sun brunch, 6pm-9pm Sun
● **PRICE:** Lunch & Brunch €21, Dinner €35, House wine €17.50
● **CREDIT CARDS:** Visa, Mastercard

● **NOTES:**
Full wheelchair access. Children welcome early evening only.

● **DIRECTIONS:**
Beside the Olympia Theatre.

MOE'S

Ian Connelly & Elaine Murphy
112 Lr Baggot Street,
Dublin 2
Tel: (01) 676 7610, Fax: 676 7619
moesdublin@hotmail.com
www.moesdublin.com

Ian Connelly and his team manage to make virtues out of the limitations of their basement, and offer excellent value for money.

Moe's has carved out a neat little niche for itself, in a part of Dublin already blessed with good rooms and good cooks. Very keen value for money keeps folk coming back, especially at lunchtime when they do a brisk trade, but it's first and foremost the personable service and a winning variant of modern international cooking which has seen Ian and Elaine sending them home happy.

The menu is wisely kept concise and seasonal – this is a small room with a very small kitchen – and what impresses is that the more adventurous dishes – chickpea and feta croquettes seasoned with turmeric, cumin and parsley, for instance – are just as well realised as the more conventional starters and mains such as smoked salmon with capers and lemon, or rib-eye steak with green beans. There is a succulence to this cooking that runs all the way through to very good desserts, all amiably served.

● **OPEN:** 12.30pm-3pm Mon-Fri, 6pm-11pm Mon-Sat
● **PRICE:** Lunch €25, Dinner €41,
House wine €18
● **CREDIT CARDS:** All major cards accepted

● **NOTES:**
No wheelchair access. Vegetarian menu.
Children welcome, but note, it's a small room,

● **DIRECTIONS:**
Corner of Baggot Street and Fitzwilliam Street.

MONTYS OF KATMANDU

Shiva Gautam
28 Eustace St, Temple Bar,
Dublin 2
Tel: (01) 670 4911 Fax: 494 4359
montys@eircom.net
www.montys.ie

Monty's serves true, creative Nepalese cookery, done with great care and affection and magical attention to detail.

Simple, modest and unassuming, Monty's of Katmandu is the kind of special gem you'd easily be tempted to keep to yourself. It's nothing to look at from the outside, plain as punch within. But Monty's cooking is exceptional, especially in light of its location in Temple Bar, a hotbed of mediocre and overpriced restaurants.

Head chef Birendra Shrestha, and head tandoori chef Ramesh Lamichane produce cooking with subtlety and precision: try a sekuwa chatpâté chicken, for example, and you taste all the elements of charcoal-grilled chicken with onions, tomatoes, chillies, lemon, masala spice mixture, and lots of fresh-chopped parsley, coriander and scallions. Prawn chata mari features tender, gingery sweet-sour prawns served on an authentically Nepali thin rice pancake. Owner Shiva Gautam's focus is on the details, and the passion for good food evident here is just darling.

● **OPEN:** Noon-2.10pm, 6pm-11.30pm Mon-Sat, 6pm-11pm Sun
● **PRICE:** Tasting menus €27-€40, House wine €18
● **CREDIT CARDS:** Visa, Mastercard, Amex

● **NOTES:**
Wheelchair access to ground floor, but not toilets. Children welcome off peak hours. Recommended for vegetarians. Special diets well catered for.

● **DIRECTIONS:**
Located directly across from the Irish Film Centre (IFC) in Temple Bar.

O'CONNELL'S

Tom & Rory O'Connell, Hazel Allen
Bewley's Aparthotel, Merrion Rd,
Ballsbridge, Dublin 4
Tel: (01) 647 3304, Fax: 647 3499
oconnellsballsbridge@eircom.net
www.oconnellsballsbridge.com

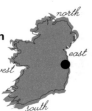

A textbook brasserie with enviably consistent food that is always underpinned by the use of the best Irish ingredients.

If Tom O'Connell and his team wanted to give up cooking, they could always make a living teaching folk how to write a menu properly. Shanagarry smoked salmon with horseradish cream. Wexford beefsteak with garlic and herb butter. Irish hereford prime steak with 3-peppercorn sauce. East Cork smoked fish plate. Salad of Gubbeen bacon. Atlantic organic salmon with cheddar cheese and mustard. The provenance of these artisan ingredients is the key note of this hugely successful brasserie, and their flavour means that all the team has to do is to keep it simple and get the food to the table. They manage that with gas in the tank: wild mussels with garlic butter breadcrumbs are spot on; spit-roast leg of lamb has a sweet purée of turnip; pan-fried sea trout with cucumber and dill butter is good, straight-ahead cookery. Good wine list, and the room has great energy.

● **OPEN:** 7am-10.30am, 12.30pm-2.30pm, 6pm-10.30pm Mon-Sat (Sat from 7.30am), 8am-11am, 12.30pm-3pm, 6pm-9.30pm Sun
● **PRICE:** Lunch €20, Dinner €30
● **CREDIT CARDS:** All major cards accepted

● **NOTES:**
Wheelchair access. Children welcome.

● **DIRECTIONS:**
Basement of the Bewley's Hotel on Merrion Road, round the corner from the RDS, and opposite the Four Seasons Hotel.

ONE PICO

Eamonn O'Reilly
5-6 Molesworth Place,
Schoolhouse Lane, Dublin 2
Tel: (01) 676 0300 Fax: 676 0411
eamonnoreilly@ireland.com
www.onepico.com

The One Pico team hit the ground running. They're still trying to catch their breath, poor things.

Eamonn O'Reilly and his team hit the ground running and they have had to keep their feet on the throttle ever since as O'Reilly's witty, fussy cooking has met with ever-greater acclaim. Part of their success is down to a truly great room – this is an ace date restaurant – and very polished service that ticks over with metronomic efficiency. But the cooking completes the circle of attraction, and the growing maturity evident in O'Reilly's work is a pleasure to behold.

He still sticks his thumb into every dish as he signs his culinary signature everywhere – a curry sauce vierge with sea bass and crushed potatoes; salmon with red onion béarnaise and candied walnuts; crab cake with bell peppers stew; leek and saffron risotto with poached egg. It is fussy food, but it works, and O'Reilly and chef Maurice Fitzgerald keep a tight grip. Ace value for money.

● **OPEN:** 12.30pm-2pm, 6pm-10pm Mon-Sat
● **PRICE:** Lunch €21-25, Dinner €40-50, House recommended wine €31.11
● **CREDIT CARDS:** All major cards accepted

● **NOTES:**
Limited wheelchair access. Children over 10 years welcome.

● **DIRECTIONS:**
Located on a small laneway, off Dawson Street, five minutes' walk from St Stephen's Green.

101 TALBOT

Margaret Duffy & Pascal Bradley
101 Talbot Street,
Dublin 1
Tel: (01) 874 5011
Fax: (01) 875 5011

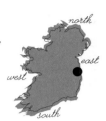

Irish cucina casalingua – true, simple domestic cooking – is the order of the day in 101 Talbot, one of the vital city addresses.

Few restaurants offer such superb value for money as the legendary 101 Talbot, but good value is only part of the story of the success of this inner-city veteran.

Pascal Bradley and Margaret Duffy run one of the most democratic, sane, sensible and dignified city restaurants. There is no hype to 101, no brashness, no slickness. Instead, there is a team of people dedicated to their work, happy to produce fine food at fine prices for an audience who respect and admire the restaurant and its food. In many ways, 101 is the sort of quiet (well, noisily quiet) place you might find in an Italian city, a restaurant that specialises in cucina casalingua – domestic cooking – for a devoted audience.

Even though the menu style is international – from spanakopita to Thai-style fish – everything has the gentle 101 signature to it.

- **OPEN:** 5pm-11pm Tue-Sat
- **PRICE:** Dinner €25, House wine €14.75
- **CREDIT CARDS:** Visa, Mastercard, Amex

- **NOTES:**
No wheelchair access. Well behaved children welcome before 8pm.

- **DIRECTIONS:**
Three minutes' walk from O'Connell Street, down Talbot Street. Look up on your right and you will see their sign. The restaurant is upstairs, on the first floor, over the shops.

POPPADOM RESTAURANT

Zerxes Ginwalla
91a Rathgar Road,
Dublin 6
Tel: (01) 490 2383
Fax: 492 3900

Zerxes Ginwalla and his team pay acute attention to every single detail in Poppadom, and it shows in special food and a special room.

Louise Kennedy glasses and water jugs. Royal Doulton china. Avoca Handweavers hand-painted cups and saucers. Lemon Street gallery prints. A wine list from Martin Moran M.W. We are a long way from bargain basement balti here, aren't we? Zerxes Ginwalla and his team work really hard to take Poppadom out of the ghetto of Indian restaurants, and their hard work pays off; this is a handsome, well-loved and seriously busy neighbourhood restaurant with great food and fine service.

Tandoori prawns with a fresh mint chutney are powerfully flavourful and typical of well-judged starters, and mains feature rare dishes such as venison tikka and duck achari, with cubes of duck meat cooked with yoghurt and onion. The vegetarian selection is especially good, and don't miss their new Newlands X take-away.

- **OPEN:** 6pm-midnight Mon-Sun
- **PRICE:** Dinner €30, House wine €17.14
- **CREDIT CARDS:** All major cards accepted

- **NOTES:**
Wheelchair access.
Children welcome.
Recommended for vegetarians.

- **DIRECTIONS:**
At the end of the Rathgar Road, opposite the Church, just near Corman's pub.

ROLY'S BISTRO

Colin O'Daly
7 Ballsbridge Terrace
Ballsbridge, Dublin 4
Tel: (01) 668 2611, Fax: 660 8535
rolysbistro@ireland.com
www.rolysbistro.com

The archetypal
powerhouse brasserie, as
alluring and enjoyable
as ever.

It is simply unthinkable to imagine Dublin without Roly's. People visiting the capital will actually make a booking to eat here before they even consider where they are going to stay for the night, that is how much of an icon destination Colin O'Daly's restaurant is.

It's a destination because no other room has the sheer energy, the wildness, the clamour of this stylish brasserie, and because Paul Cartwright's cooking is so well judged, so flavourful and just-what-I-wanted. We have remarked before on the fact that what Roly's does should be impossible; they serve high quality food to huge numbers of people, yet the quality rarely dips, and the cooking can be spiffingly splendid: subtle potato soup with tarragon; lovely Kerry lamb and vegetable pie; Peking duck with roasted sweet potato; raspberry pavlova with white chocolate soup. Value is great, and Roly's is irresistible.

- **OPEN:** noon-3pm, 6pm-10pm Mon-Sun
- **PRICE:** Lunch €17.71, Dinner €40, House wine €17.70
- **CREDIT CARDS:** All major cards accepted

- **NOTES:**
Full wheelchair access.
Children welcome.

- **DIRECTIONS:**
Corner of Ballsbridge and Herbert Park, just down from the RDS.

SHANAHAN'S ON THE GREEN

John Shanahan
119 St Stephen's Green,
Dublin 2
Tel: (01) 407 0939,
Fax: 407 0940

John Shanahan's high-concept restaurant, with high prices to match, has been one of the city's great successes.

You can hardly get a table in John Shanahan's big, brassy steak house, a fact which, given all the competition on his doorstep and his stone-me! sky-high prices, is the proof of just how well achieved this high-concept restaurant actually is.

People like it because Shanahan's has a style of service that is seductively impressive. You feel cossetted and pampered, and somehow all the money you are spending seems well spent: in culinary terms, it's a food lover's spa treatment, an immersion tank of comfort whilst your wallet gets a damn good massage also.

Meat is the thing, meticulously sourced and prepared Irish Angus beef which is sweet as sin, and always cooked as ordered: you will get that black and blue here if you ask. But their attention to detail is everywhere, so for that big, big date, it's Shanahan's.

- **OPEN:** 6pm-10pm Mon-Sat
- **PRICE:** Dinner €65
- **CREDIT CARDS:** All major cards accepted.

- **NOTES:**
No wheelchair access.
Children - no facilities.
Reservations recommended.

- **DIRECTIONS:**
Overlooking St Stephen's Green. On the west side between Eircom House and The College of Surgeons.

THE TEA ROOM

Bono, The Edge, Harry Crosbie
The Clarence Hotel
6-8 Wellington Quay, Dublin 2
Tel: (01) 407 0800, Fax: 407 0820
reservations@theclarence.ie
www.theclarence.ie

Antony Ely's beautifully measured cooking is top notch. Can't say the same for the music.

Antony Ely is a great cook, and he enjoys one of the city's most beautiful rooms to cook for: whatever other contenders there may be, The Tea Room gets our prize as the great date restaurant, and with service now much more confident than in the recent past, TTR is hot
This is marvellously enjoyable cooking, with a serene signature style that is totally winning: potato and bacon cakes with curly kale and caper sauce; braised neck of lamb with Agen prunes and cocotte potatoes; sea bass with a tarte fine of ceps; squab pigeon with choucroute and a little roast foie gras; nice cheffy dishes such as roast loin, sliced rump and confit belly of pork with an assortment of garnishes. Desserts are just as clever and confident: homemade vanilla yogurt with apple crumble; excellent pineapple tarte tatin. The music they choose to play, however, is utterly inappropriate for the room.

● **OPEN:** 7am-11am, 12.30pm-2.30pm, 6.30pm-10.30pm
Mon-Sun (On Sun there is brunch)
● **PRICE:** Dinner €49.50, House wine €27
● **CREDIT CARDS:** All major cards accepted

● **NOTES:**
Full wheelchair access.
Children welcome.

● **DIRECTIONS:**
In the city centre, overlooking the River Liffey,
approximately 150metres up from Ha'penny Bridge,
south of river, 30-45 minutes from Dublin Airport.

THORNTON'S

Kevin & Muriel Thornton
1 Portobello Road, Dublin 8
Tel: (01) 454 9067
Fax: 453 2947
thorntons@iol.ie

Transcendent cooking from Kevin Thornton and his team is one of Dublin's glories.

Kevin Thornton is the most garlanded Irish chef at work today, and most likely the most dedicated, with a devotion to the kitchen that raises his work to the status of vocation.

But if the rosettes and the hard graft make Thornton's sound like a place that could be all too serious, rest assured that this cook has plenty of wit and wonder in his work. It's not unusual, for instance, for Thornton and his team to cook a service where every single dish (yes, every single dish) will be improvised and personalised. His devoted clientele trust this modest man so much that they glance at the menus, but then let the chef ignore them: they want it the way he wants it.

This sort of trust makes for a restaurant with a truly unique relationship between chef and customer, an umbilical connection that allows this great cook to push the culinary boundaries. Thornton's is one of the truly sublime dining experiences, an expensive, glorious piece of culinary theatre.

- **OPEN:** 12.30pm-1.45pm Fri, 7pm-10pm Tue-Sat
- **PRICE:** Lunch €36.50, Dinner €80, House wine €19
- **CREDIT CARDS:** All major cards accepted.

- **NOTES:**
No wheelchair access (though happy to help). Children welcome, high chair.

- **DIRECTIONS:**
Overlooking Grand Canal, near Harold's Cross bridge.

TRIBECA

Trevor Browne & Gerard Foote
65 Ranelagh Village,
Dublin 6
Tel: (01) 497 4174
Fax: 491 1584

It took just five days for Tribeca to be packed lunch and dinner.
Eat those wings and see just how they did it.

It took just five days for this restaurant to be packed at both lunch and dinner, a new paradigm of success in the food world. And that success is based — wait for this — on spicy chicken wings. Here they are once again, as expertly and irresistibly done as they have been in the Elephant & Castle for the last decade, where Trevor Browne and Gerard Foote began. Like the wings, Tribeca's food is straightforward, based on good ingredients, and unpretentious: salmon burger with grilled onions and thick, salty chips; hot and sour coconut prawns with egg noodles; spaghetti with aubergine, tomato and ricotta; sweetcorn chowder with roasted red pepper and coriander; excellent sandwiches and good brunch omelettes; figure-bustin' ice creams. Large mirrors make the room seem enormous, blue banquettes match the baby blue T-shirts of the staff and the sounds are ace.

- **OPEN:** 8.30am-11.30am Mon-Fri, noon-11pm Mon-Sun
- **PRICE:** Menu €8.50-35, House wine €16.95
- **CREDIT CARDS:** Visa, Mastercard

- **NOTES:**
Wheelchair access. Children welcome.
No reservations taken at weekends, but do take them on the day, Mon-Fri.

- **DIRECTIONS:**
Next door to the Ulster Bank on Ranelagh road, just up from the triangle.

THE ARCHWAY

Brendan O'Sullivan, Regis Martin, Anita Martin
3 Victoria Place, Galway,
Co Galway Tel: (091) 563693,
Fax: 563074 archway@indigo.ie
www.archway.ie

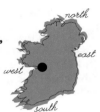

Already a staple of the Galway scene, the calm and formal Archway is a poised counterpoint to the raucous city ambience.

Maybe it is precisely because the way in which Regis Martin and his team work, exploiting that quintessentially measured French style of cooking and service which combines formality with stateliness, that The Archway has succeeded so well. The way they do things here is a direct contrast to the informality which underpins virtually every other place to eat in boisterous Galway city, so it's no surprise locals like a taste of calm consideration every now and again. Certainly, they find it here, along with clever, well-grounded cooking that takes its cue very firmly from French classical cooking: peppercorn sauce with beef; vermouth sauces for fish and shellfish, perfectly rendered duck confit and melt-in-the-mouth foie gras, along with archetype desserts such as crème brûlée which are done to perfection. The room is elegant, the service perhaps a little too reserved.

● **OPEN:** 12.30pm-1.45pm, 7pm-9.45pm Tue-Sat. Open Sun on bank holiday weekends only
● **PRICE:** Lunch €19.68, Dinner €39, House wine €23
● **CREDIT CARDS:** All major cards accepted

● **NOTES:**
No wheelchair access. Reservation recommended.

● **DIRECTIONS:**
In a recess just off Eyre Square, directly across from the main tourist office in the centre of the city.

BALLYNAHINCH CASTLE

Patrick O'Flaherty
Ballinafad, Recess, Co Galway
Tel: (095) 31006, Fax: 31006
bhinch@iol.ie
www.ballynahinch-castle.com

Isn't that Michael Eisner over there, in the cycling shorts?
He knows a good thing when he finds it, doesn't he.

A democratic castle sounds like the quintessential oxymoron, but Ballynahinch shows that those two ideas can live happily side by side.

Billionaires and bikers come here; locals and high-rolling weekenders from the cities; oul fellas drink in the bar and console failed dotcommers. The world and his wife all come to Ballynahinch and, aside from the craic, Robert Webster's cooking is one of the principal attractions.

Mister Webster cooks just the right sort of food for this beautiful dining room (and it really is one of the prettiest in the country). Fish and game dominate, of course, as this is a huntin', shootin' and fishin' destination, but there is grace and simplicity and a winning style in all his food, along with a light touch that matches the carefree spirit of this beautiful destination. Great staff under the genial guidance of Patrick O'Flaherty complete the magic.

- **OPEN:** 6.30pm-9pm Mon-Sun. Closed Feb.
- **PRICE:** Dinner €42
- **CREDIT CARDS:** All major credit cards accepted.

- **NOTES:**
Lunch available in the bar. Limited wheelchair access. Parking in grounds. Children welcome, babysitting, cots.

- **DIRECTIONS:**
Approximately 4.5 hours from Dublin. As you approach Galway take signs for Clifden or Oughterard (N59). After Maam Cross, then Recess you will see the signs for Ballynahinch Castle. 3.5 hours from Shannon.

HIGH MOORS

Hugh & Eileen Griffin
Dooneen,
Clifden,
Co Galway
Tel: (095) 21342

In High Moors, Hugh and Eileen take the concept of "homegrown" to new heights.

Hugh and Eileen Griffin's restaurant is in the sitting room of their bungalow, high up on the hill a mile outside the busy town of Clifden in Connemara. Hugh serves the food at dinnertime, and grows the vegetables and fruits in his polytunnel and vegetable patch, down the hill in their garden. Eileen takes the bookings, and cooks all the food on her Aga in her kitchen, starting in the morning with breads and desserts (don't miss the fruit crumble, the one the French go doolalley for). The cooking is dreamy and delicious: terrific herb-stuffed mussels are briny and breadcrumby; local Connemara lamb can be a sweet roasted loin or their trademark spicy lamb shanks; Carna Bay scallops with a basil sauce are subtly saline; and like everyone else you never think you will eat that big dish of vegetables, but blow me if there isn't so much as a frond of fennel left when the plates are lifted. Terrific.

● **OPEN:** 7pm-9.30pm Wed-Sun. Closed Oct-May
● **PRICE:** Dinner €32, House wine €16
● **CREDIT CARDS:** Visa, Mastercard, Amex

● **NOTES:**
Wheelchair access.
Children welcome, high chair.

● **DIRECTIONS:**
Go 100metres on the Ballyconeely Road, and you will see the signpost. Travel for another 1km up this side road until you get to the restaurant. There are two or three signs.

NIMMOS

Harriet Leander
Spanish Arch,
Galway,
Co Galway
Tel: (091) 561114

The mad, clamorous electrified energy of Galway is found right here in Nimmo's.

The smart local money all heads down to Nimmo's, Harriet Leander's inspiring wine bar and restaurant, hard by the famous Spanish Arch at the Corrib River. The buzz is quintessential Galway: raucous, fun, and quite loveable, improvised and even inspired, which might also describe the food.

The fish soup is intoxicatingly spicy; smoked salmon salad has excellent fish and fine organic leaves; aubergine bake sounds uninspiring but is packed with comforting, enjoyable flavours; boeuf bourguignon is a modest dish of beef cubes and a rich wine sauce with plenty of spuds to mop up, and Parmesan chicken balances sweet and sharp flavours with ease. Desserts are bought in from the legendary Goya's bakery in town, so don't miss the lemon meringue and plum tarts, and there are some splendid Spanish bottles of red on the list. Just darling.

● **OPEN:** 12.30pm-3pm, 6.60pm-10pm Tue-Sun. Wine bar open all day. From 6pm Sun.
● **PRICE:** Lunch €10-15, Dinner €30, House wine €16
● **CREDIT CARDS:** Visa, Mastercard

● **NOTES:**
Live music on Sunday. No wheelchair access. Children, no facilities.

● **DIRECTIONS:**
The old stone building directly underneath the Spanish Arch, across from the Jury's hotel in the centre of the city.

10 RESTAURANTS
WITH GREAT SERVICE

1
ALDEN'S
BELFAST, NORTHERN IRELAND

2
CHAPTER ONE
DUBLIN, CO DUBLIN

3
THE CORNCRAKE
CARNDONAGH, CO DONEGAL

4
L'ECRIVAIN
DUBLIN, CO DUBLIN

5
LA MARINE
ROSSLARE, CO WEXFORD

6
THE MERMAID
DUBLIN, CO DUBLIN

7
RESTAURANT DAVID NORRIS
TRALEE, CO KERRY

8
SHANAHAN'S
DUBLIN, CO DUBLIN

9
SHANKS
BANGOR, NORTHERN IRELAND

10
SUN KEE
BELFAST, NORTHERN IRELAND

ALLO'S BAR & BISTRO

**Armel Whyte & Helen Mullane
41 Church Street,
Listowel, Co Kerry
Tel: (068) 22880
Fax: 22803
www.allos.ie**

The bar and bistro
from heaven, so beam us
up, Scottie, we're ready to
ascend.

A bar, bistro and townhouse might make Helen Mullane
and Armel Whyte's operation sound grand, but in reality
it's a petite place in the petite, pretty town of Listowel.
Ms Mullane minds front of house and bakes terrific sweet
things, and Mr Whyte cooks some of the savviest modern
Irish food you can eat. His cooking is significant because
he refines an appreciation of Irish cooking into something
modern, but never loses the ethos of a true country
cook. Mrs Murphy's ducks will have a potato stuffing; a bar
lunch might offer boiled ham with cabbage and a parsley
sauce; dinner might be turbot with a tarragon beurre
blanc; a spoonsome dessert of pineapple gateau with
home-made custard is purest age-old fare.
Mullane and Whyte are blessed with good taste, and the
bar, the bistro and the rooms are unique, the food blessed
with flavours any Irish chef would be proud of.

- **OPEN:** Noon-9.15pm Tue-Sat (closed 7pm Mon)
- **PRICE:** Lunch €16, Dinner €40, House wine €18
- **CREDIT CARDS:** Visa, Mastercard, Amex

- **NOTES:**
Reservations recommended. Wheelchair access.
Children welcome, high chair.

- **DIRECTIONS:**
1 hour's drive from Limerick on the N69. Allo's is in the
centre of Listowel, opposite the Garda station.

THE CHART HOUSE

Jim McCarthy
The Mall, Dingle,
Co Kerry
Tel: (066) 915 2255, Fax: 915 2255
charthse@iol.ie
www.charthousedingle.com

A room that has a welcome all about it, and don't miss the fab local black pudding from Annascaul.

Jim McCarthy's Chart House restaurant swiftly became the destination address in busy Dingle after opening, and it has stayed that way ever since. The gracious and charming manner of the host, a genial room which suits the holiday spirit of the town, and some sure-fire cooking means this is the place everyone books before they head down the peninsula for some r'n'r.

The food, as the professionals might say, is tasty, first and foremost: Annascaul black pudding in filo with gingered apples (don't miss this: Annascaul is one of the very best black puddings you can eat); fillet steak with bubble and squeak; Kerry lamb with ratatouille and grilled polenta; pork fillet stuffed with apricot; brill with garlic spinach and smoky bacon; rhubarb compote with vanilla bean sauce. If you're tired of this cooking then you are tired of life, for it has a winning energy and welcome in it.

- **OPEN:** 6.30pm-10pm (closed 7 Jan & Valentine's)
- **PRICE:** Dinner €32, House wine €15.50
- **CREDIT CARDS:** Visa, Mastercard, Laser

- **NOTES:**
Full wheelchair access. Children welcome.
Recommended for coeliacs (one member of staff is coeliac and so is well prepared for this request).
Importing a selection of South African wines.

- **DIRECTIONS:**
Left at the roundabout as you approach Dingle from Killarney.

RESTAURANT DAVID NORRIS

David Norris
Ivy House,
Ivy Terrace,
Tralee,
Co Kerry
Tel: (066) 718 5654

ONly FAIR - SERVICE POOR !

Local boy makes good with
stylish, mature cooking that
has created a vital new
destination in Kerry.

David Norris has returned to his birthplace, and has
finally given Tralee the destination address it has needed
for years. For here be serious, stylish cooking, served with
great care, in a neat upstairs room. Mr Norris' food is
measured and mature, and he signs everything he does
with considerable deliciousness. His confit of duck with
pickled walnuts is exceptionally fine; whilst with pan-fried
scallops with a sauce made from the corals, he shows
deftness and deliciousness in complete accord. Crisp
Serrano ham and a pitch-perfect potato rösti complete a
dish that shows all the merits of this kitchen. He is no
slouch with desserts either, as a perfect lime and liquorice
parfait with poached pears and a caramel sauce shows.
Set menus are very good value for money, the wine list
will surely improve along with the music, and at last
something to get excited about in Tralee.

- **OPEN:** 6.30pm-10pm Tue-Sat
- **PRICE:** Dinner €38, House wine €17.95
- **CREDIT CARDS:** Visa, Mastercard, Amex

- **NOTES:**
No wheelchair access.
Children welcome, but no facilities.

- **DIRECTIONS:**
An upstairs restaurant, just across the road from the
Brandon Hotel, facing Siamsa Tira.

GABY'S

Geert and Marie Maes
27 High Street,
Killarney,
Co Kerry
Tel: (064) 32519,
Fax: 32747

Thirty years a cookin', and Geert Maes and his team are as fleet of foot and finger as they have ever been.

Whilst quite a lot of the style and the menu and the manner of service of Gaby's seems quite old-fashioned in our relentlessly fashion-conscious age, there is nothing retro about the cooking Geert Maes and his team manage to knock out in this bustlingly busy restaurant. They make a tempura of prawns, for instance, which any Vong restaurant would envy, so deft and precise is the tempura batter, whilst scallops served with champ is the sort of curious choice of ingredients that is rewarded with complete success. But that mixture of the ruddy and the ethereal is shown again with terrific sea bass with Savoy cabbage and bacon, savvy cooking that is judged just right thanks to an orange-scented beurre blanc. Vegetables and desserts are less assured and could be worked on, but the enthusiasm of the staff under Marie Maes is completely winning, and the wine list is a bibulous treat.

- **OPEN:** 6pm-10pm Mon-Sat
- **PRICE:** Dinner €32, House wine €25
- **CREDIT CARDS:** Visa, Mastercard, Amex, Diners

- **NOTES:**
Wheelchair access with assistance. Closed Christmas and mid Feb-mid-Mar. Children welcome.

- **DIRECTIONS:**
In the centre of Killarney, just down from the market cross.

MULCAHY'S

**Bruce Mulachy
16 Henry Street,
Kenmare,
Co Kerry
Tel: (064) 42383**

A funky room with stylish fusion food, Mulcahy's is another complement to the great gastronomic grotto of Kenmare.

Bruce Mulcahy's restaurant, with its fusion-influenced food and its whacky dining room (holes in the walls, clashing colours, waves of candles) has added a valuable note to Kenmare. Mulcahy learnt his fusion in Australia before returning home, and it shows in touches such as green tea anglaise with pannacotta, or a fine wild garlic bread. He wheels it out in the unusual mixture of serving scallops with red grapes and leeks, or with quenelles of herbed, marinated goat's cheese. Without his sure touch, such flamboyance could easily get lost, but there is discipline and subtlety to his work. Above all, he likes flavour, and it shows with john dory with a demon mussel cream, and a French lemon tart with amaretto cream which is pure ooh!aah! territory. Service is precise and professional, prices are fair, and here is another more-than-worthy Kenmare contender.

● **OPEN:** from 6.30pm Thur-Mon low season, Wed-Mon high season. Closed 2 weeks in Jan and Nov, otherwise open all year.
● **PRICE:** Dinner €30-35, House wine €16.50
● **CREDIT CARDS:** Visa, Mastercard

● **NOTES:**
Six-course tasting menu Jun-Sept, €48. Wheelchair access. Children welcome for first sitting.

● **DIRECTIONS:**
In the centre of Kenmare, on the left as you travel down the one-way street, coming from Glengarriff.

VERY GOOD ★★★ FOOD AND SERVICE

PACKIE'S ✳

Tom & Maura Foley O'Connell
Henry Street,
Kenmare,
Co Kerry
Tel: (064) 41508, Fax: 42135

Cooking this simple reveals nothing less than genius, and genius is what Maura Foley deals in.

The menu in Packie's reads like it was written by a child: potato pancakes with garlic butter. Smoked trout mousse with toast. Scallops with pesto. Beef braised in Guinness. Chicken with coriander and lime. Brill with a mustard sauce. Dover sole with cream and brandy.

This isn't restaurant cooking, is it? And the anwer is; no, it is Maura Foley's cooking, and there isn't a nobler, more inspired or more inspirational style of cooking to be found anywhere in Ireland. This food is full of wonder.

Where others overstate, Mrs Foley understates. Where other show off, she lets the flavours speak for themselves. Culinary technique seems to be absent from this food: it is almost as if it is in some ways a "found" cuisine, where flavours are revealed rather than created.

And there is no cooking like it: profound, dignified, simple, potent. Genius is not an overstatement.

- ● **OPEN:** 5.30pm-10pm Tue-Sat. Closed Nov-Easter
- ● **PRICE:** Dinner €30-35, House wine €16
- ● **CREDIT CARDS:** Visa, Mastercard

- ● **NOTES:**
Wheelchair access (but not to toilets). Children welcome, high chair.

- ● **DIRECTIONS:**
In the centre of Kenmare, the first street you meet when coming from the direction of Glengarriff.

SHEEN FALLS LODGE

Adriaan Bartels
Kenmare, Co Kerry
Tel: (064) 41600
Fax: (064) 41386
info@sheenfallslodge.ie
www.sheenfallslodge.ie

Chris Farrell's cooking has propelled the SFL into a new league of delicious creativity.

It might seem a small thing to remark upon, but Chris Farrell and his team in the SFL cook what is probably the finest, most considered vegetarian menu in the country. But it's not a small thing, it's a typical thing, for the cooking here – indeed the entire m.o of the SF – is care, concern, making sure you have what you want.

The cooking works with suggestible layers of flavour – john dory will have a confit of fennel, an artichoke purée and a citrus cream, for instance – but restraint and attention to detail means that the food comes out singing all from the same hymn sheet. Some smoked belly of pork served with roast squab is inspired, their own smoked salmon with cucumber jelly and beluga is perfect. Desserts are excellent, in particular a fantastic, wobbly pannacotta. Fantastic wine list, high prices that are worth every cent, and even a pianist who likes some Schubert.

- **OPEN:** Open Dinner. Closed Jan
- **PRICE:** Dinner €60
- **CREDIT CARDS:** All major cards accepted.

- **NOTES:**
Recommended for vegetarians. Full wheelchair access. Parking in grounds. Children welcome, babysitting, cots, outdoor play area. Bar open for lunch, and Oscars Bistro serves more informal cooking.

- **DIRECTIONS:**
35 miles from Kerry Airport, and 60 miles from Cork airport. From Kenmare, leave on the Glengarriff road, and take first turn left after the suspension bridge.

THE BALLYMORE INN

Barry & Georgina O'Sullivan
Ballymore Eustace,
Co Kildare
Tel: (045) 864585,
Fax: 864747

Is this the best meat cookery in Ireland? Probably, but everything else in TBI is just as good.

Not many people know that there is an unwritten code amongst food writers that, when judging a restaurant, you always choose something other than the steak dishes. Other ingredients offer more of a chance for the kitchen to show what it can do, is the logic, even if restaurants actually cook steak brilliantly.

Problem is, ask a Bridgestone editor to head down to Ballymore Eustace to bring you right up to speed with what Georgina O'Sullivan and her team are doing in the Ballymore Inn, and you will get a report back which will spend all its time arguing the merits of the sirloin over the fillet. Asking a food lover to come here and not to eat meat is, frankly, a bit like asking Casanova to babysit your teenage daughters: beyond temptation. The meat cookery is amazing. But, let's be fair; so is everything else, which is why it is so difficult to get a table here.

● **OPEN:** 12.30pm-3pm Mon, 12.30pm-3pm, 6pm-9pm Tue-Thur, 12.30pm-9pm Fri-Sat (kitchen closes 8pm in bar and kitchen closed Sun and bank hols)
● **PRICE:** Lunch €13-19, Dinner €25-30
● **CREDIT CARDS:** Visa, Mastercard, Amex

● **NOTES:**
Full wheelchair access. Children welcome.

● **DIRECTIONS:**
From Dublin, take the N81, signpost Tallaght. Turn right 2-3 miles after Blessington, signed to Ballymore Eustace, and the Inn is in the centre of the village on the right hand side.

ZUNI

**Paul & Paula Byrne, Sandra &
Alan McDonald
26 Patrick St, Kilkenny
Tel: (056) 23999, Fax: 56400
info@zuni.ie
www.zuni.ie**

Zuni has stolen the hearts, minds and tummies of hip Kilkenny folk, with a brilliant formula at great prices.

It can all look a bit made-to-measure, the Zuni formula that has wowed the beautiful city of Kilkenny. There's the moody bar with its leather sofas and low lighting; there's the must-have open-view kitchen; there's the minimalist dining room; there's the modern-by-numbers menu with its polystylist food: blackened chicken Caesar; confit of duck with noodles; Thai fish cakes; tandoori roasted cod; sweet chilli chicken and king prawn chow mein.
Yet, somehow, it all works. Twin identical sisters Paula and Sandra and husbands Alan and Paul power this impressive restaurant with rooms, but the solid delivery of very tasty food explains why it works. Those Thai fish cakes are good; the barbary duck with apple mash is full-on with flavour, and only a polenta and blackberry cake is less well realised. Service is swift and charming, prices are keen, and the A to Z of Kilkenny are in Zuni.

- **OPEN:** 12.30pm-2.30pm, 6.30pm-10pm Tue-Sun
- **PRICE:** Dinner €30-40
- **CREDIT CARDS:** Visa, Mastercard, Amex, Laser

- **NOTES:**
Full wheelchair access.
Children welcome, cots but no other facilities.

- **DIRECTIONS:**
In the city centre (around the corner from Kilkenny Castle).

THE WILD GEESE

David Foley & Julie Randles,
The Wild Geese Restaurant,
Adare, Co Limerick
Tel: (061) 396451, Fax: 396451
wildgeese@indigo.ie

Limerick's destination restaurant sails on, enjoying the spirited cooking and spirited hospitality of David and Julie.

The rooms of Rose Cottage, home to the Wild Geese restaurant, are a place of such seductive enchantment that David Foley could cook gruel and Julie Randles could behave like Peter Langan, and folk would probably still be happy to head back to this lovely restaurant in this loveliest of villages. Happily, David Foley is a great cook, and Julie Randles is as genial a host as you will find, so they complement the enchantment of the rooms by their own culinary magic and quiet charm.

David Foley's food has a ethereal lightness to it, which means that he can place lots of ingredients on the plate – monkfish with crabmeat and creamed spinach with a pepper coulis, or canon of lamb with his own black pudding wrapped in pastry, for instance – without ever risking losing his way. He is accomplished, a professional, and that professionalism is everywhere in the Wild Geese.

- **OPEN:** 6.30pm-10pm Tue-Sat
- **PRICE:** Dinner €42, House wine €20.50
- **CREDIT CARDS:** Visa, Mastercard, Amex, Diners

- **NOTES:**
Wheelchair access to ground level only, not to bathrooms. Children welcome before 7.30pm.

- **DIRECTIONS:**
From Limerick, take the N21, signposted to Killarney/Tralee. The restaurant is in the centre of Adare, directly opposite the Dunraven Arms Hotel.

CASTLE LESLIE

Sammy Leslie & Ultan Bannon
Glaslough, Co Monaghan
Tel: (047) 88109, Fax: 88109
info@castleleslie.com
www.castleleslie.com

Noel McMeel, one of the finest young Irish chefs, is cooking at full tilt and with full flavour in the grand Castle Leslie.

Noel McMeel has rediscovered the fantastic culinary groove that made him such a powerhouse figure in Northern Irish cooking, and Sammy Leslie's big old pile, Castle Leslie, is proving to be just the right forum for this gifted cook to show exactly what he is capable of.

There is technique aplenty in his work - particularly his intricate desserts - but first and foremost he takes care of flavour: if the food is good enough to gaze at, it's even better to eat, especially the game dishes which originate from the estate.

Choosing is an agony: Thai-style gateau of crab? Sea bream with sun-dried tomato risotto? Roast goose with herb risotto? Confit duck with redcurrant and aniseed? Be reckless, and go for the tasting menus here, for then you see a naturally gifted chef at full tilt, and it's a pure thrill. Monaghan arise! Your hour is here.

- **OPEN:** Weekends and holidays Jan-May, Sept-Dec. Open for Christmas. Open daily May 18-Sept 14.
- **PRICE:** Dinner €44, House wine €19
- **CREDIT CARDS:** Visa, Mastercard

- **NOTES:**
The castle is not suited to wheelchairs, but wheelchair bookings welcomed in restaurant (ground floor, few steps to front door). Bookings not taken for under 18s.

- **DIRECTIONS:**
Two hours from Dublin off the N2. Just under two hours from Belfast on the Armagh/Monaghan Rd. Very detailed directions from Dublin and Belfast can be emailed or faxed.

THE NUREMORE HOTEL

Julie Gilhooly
Nuremore Hotel & Country Club,
Carrickmacross, Co Monaghan
Tel: (042) 966 1438, Fax: 966 1853
nuremore@eircom.net
www.nuremore-hotel.ie

Ray McArdle is knocking 'em dead in the Nuremore with seriously ambitious cooking from his seriously pricey kitchen.

With a million-euro-plus kitchen built for him, Ray McArdle was always going to be expected to come out with all culinary guns blazing, and the pressure was always going to be intense to produce the goods. Fear not, McArdle has made the leap from busy brasserie chef - he was the mainstay of Deane's Brasserie in Belfast - to serious cutting-edge cook, and with gas in the tank. This is very, very exciting food.

It's lavish, too: layered terrine of teal and foie gras served with a glossy, sticky, slightly saline Madeira and teal jus is just to whet the appetite, then ballotine of chicken, or stunning tortellini of lobster, langoustines and leeks, served with sliced truffle and bisque, shows just how ambitious this kitchen is. Lamb with Clonakilty black pudding and artichokes, or salmon with baby fennel and raviolo of lobster, are plush but have a restraint that means they are light and zesty rather than indulgent. The Nuremore promises much, and delivers.

- **OPEN:** 12.30pm-2.30pm, 6.30pm-9.30pm Mon-Sun
- **PRICE:** Dinner €49, House wine €19.50
- **CREDIT CARDS:** Visa, Mastercard, Amex, Diners

- **NOTES:**
Wheelchair access. Children, no special facilities.
Vegetarian menu always available.

- **DIRECTIONS:**
Situated on the N2, 80k from Dublin, 1.5k south of Carrickmacross.

CROMLEACH LODGE

Christy & Moira Tighe
Castlebaldwin, via Boyle
Co Sligo
Tel: (071) 65155, Fax: 65455
info@cromleach.com
www.cromleach.com

Moira Tighe and her all-girl kitchen team continue to pull out all the culinary stops in County Sligo with beautiful cooking.

They take such care with all the details of their cooking, do Moira Tighe and her team of girls, that what they achieve with their food has a transcendent quality about it. There is a goodness found in this food that feeds the soul as well as the appetite, and we feel it is perhaps this holistic sense which you find in the food that provokes so many people to conclude that the food they enjoy here is amongst the most absorbing and delicious food you can eat.

Curiously for an all-woman team, the food is quite cheffy – there are paupiettes and roulades and layered dishes and soufflés and trios and noisettes to match any starry male team – but the culinary thread is never lost in the complexity, and the cooking shines with true flavours, textures and goodness. The desserts have always been a benchmark, the decor always a subject of disagreement.

- **OPEN:** 7pm-8.30pm Mon-Sat, 6.30pm-8pm Sun
- **PRICE:** Dinner €55, House wine €21
- **CREDIT CARDS:** All major cards accepted

- **NOTES:**
Wheelchair access (only with assistance).
Children welcome.
Recommended for vegetarians.

- **DIRECTIONS:**
Signposted from Castlebaldwin on the N4. Three hours from Shannon airport, Dublin and Belfast.

BROCKA-ON-THE-WATER

**Anthony & Anne Gernon
Kilgarvan Quay,
Ballinderry,
Co Tipperary
Tel: (067) 22038**

Brocka is one of the most charming, loveable and disarming Irish restaurants.

Critics don't have favourite restaurants, but if you quizzed them about the ideal restaurant, chances are the reply would go like this: The restaurant would be more like a private house than a formal place. It would be family-run, by a couple of generations. Décor would be subtle but memorable, details would actually be designed for individual customers. The food would be intensely seasonal, the menu short, and signature dishes which can't be cooked by anyone else would be the mainstay.

Nope, it's not some little tratt somewhere in the Marches, or a tucked-away place in Lisbon or Palermo. We are talking about one of the truly great Irish restaurants: Brocka-on-the-Water. This is how Nancy, Anne and Anthony do things: they cook and create like artists, not mere restaurateurs, and this is everyone's dream restaurant. Bliss.

- **OPEN:** 7pm-10pm Mon-Sat
- **PRICE:** Dinner €38, House wine €19
- **CREDIT CARDS:** No credit cards

- **NOTES:**
Full wheelchair access. Booking essential off season. Children welcome, high chair.

- **DIRECTIONS:**
On Kilgarvan Quay on the Lough Derg Drive, half way between Nenagh and Portumna.

CHEZ HANS

**Hans Peter Matthiae
& Jason Matthiae
Cashel,
Co Tipperary
Tel: (062) 61177**

The beautiful Chez Hans opened in 1968, and has sailed serenely through the years with consistently delicious cooking.

Son Jason Matthiae has succeeded his dad at the stoves in Chez Hans, this splendid restaurant housed in an old deconsecrated church, which has been a staple of the Irish restaurant scene for almost three and half decades. The staple diet of Chez Hans has always been impeccable fish and shellfish cookery, and a winning way with Irish beef and lamb that manages to appeal both to trenchermen Tipperary types and would-be sophisticates. Flavour has always been paramount here, along with the use of the best ingredients. Jason then simply shows them some culinary tricks – a herb crust for local lamb which is roasted; escargot butter for lobster; a Cashel Blue stuffing for free-range chicken; quail en croûte with Madeira – whilst the dessert team come up trumps every time, and everyone, but everyone, leaves happy.

- **OPEN:** 6.30pm-10pm Tue-Sat
- **PRICE:** Dinner €40, House wine €21
- **CREDIT CARDS:** Visa, Mastercard

- **NOTES:**
Wheelchair access.
Children welcome.

- **DIRECTIONS:**
Just beside the Rock of Cashel, and clearly signposted from the Dublin-Cork road.

CLIFFORD'S AT THE BELL

Michael & Deirdre Clifford
Cahir
Co Tipperary
Tel: (052) 43232

One of Ireland's most imaginative
and important chefs continues to
deliver the goods in the centre of
lucky Cahir.

Michael Clifford's premises at The Bell may be modest –
a couple of pretty rooms on two floors above the pub of
the same name, just off the Square in the centre of Cahir
– but don't let the modesty blind you to the fact that here
is one of the master modern Irish chefs, a cook with a
range of signature dishes who continues to explore and
exploit the use of artisan ingredients.

What is so impressive about Mr Clifford's work is his
combination of rusticity with finesse, a style few others
have managed just as well as this cook can. Lamb's liver
and kidney are delicately handled, but paired with a ruddy
purée of root vegetables; his gateau of Clonakilty black
pudding somehow makes this earthy ingredient ethereal;
and few people cook lentils and other pulses with the
same lightness and sureness. Lovely desserts, fine service.

- **OPEN:** 6.30pm-10.30pm Tue-Sun
- **PRICE:** Dinner €40, House wine €19.05
- **CREDIT CARDS:** Visa, Mastercard

- **NOTES:**
No wheelchair access.
Children welcome.

- **DIRECTIONS:**
Just off the square in Cahir, over The Bell pub.

LEGENDS RESTAURANT

Michael & Rosemary O'Neill
The Kiln, Cashel, Co Tipperary
Tel: (062) 61292
info@legendsguesthouse.com
www.legendsguesthouse.com

Michael O'Neill deserves to be a better known chef: the cooking in Legends is quite splendid.

Legends is a little gem of a restaurant, with a professional panache that virtually guarantees a great time.

Michael O'Neill's food is utterly logical, with no extraneous touches, and a sure focus on whizz-bang flavours: chilled crab salad with marinated cucumber is a perfect starter; baked Cashel Blue cheese in filo with poached pear and walnuts is classic and executed with respect. Roast saddle of rabbit (the dish of 2002) with a wild mushroom stuffing is wonderfully tender, a cream peppercorn sauce light as a feather. Seared scallops with braised leeks and a chive cream sauce shows the same mature assurance as the meat and game cookery. To prove he doesn't put a foot wrong, cracking desserts of passion fruit pavlova and crisp and melting crème brûlée bring a wonderful culinary experience to a rousing end. Great service, unbelievable views of the Rock of Cashel.

● **OPEN:** 6.30pm-9.30pm Mon-Sun, closed two weeks in Nov & two weeks in Feb
● **PRICE:** Dinner €30-34
● **CREDIT CARDS:** Visa, Mastercard

● **NOTES:**
No wheelchair access.
No children under 10 years.

● **DIRECTIONS:**
At the northern end of Cashel, take the R660 travelling in the direction of Holy Cross. The house is 40 yards on the left, under the shadow of the Rock.

10 RESTAURANTS
TO BE SEEN IN

1

AQUA
HOWTH, CO DUBLIN

2

BANG CAFÉ
DUBLIN, CO DUBLIN

3

BUGGY'S GLENCAIRN INN
GLENCAIRN, CO WATERFORD

4

HALO
DUBLIN, CO DUBLIN

5

NIMMO'S
GALWAY, CO GALWAY

6

ONE PICO
DUBLIN, CO DUBLIN

7

OTTO'S CREATIVE CATERING
DUNWORLEY, CO CORK

8

POWERSFIELD HOUSE
DUNGARVAN, CO WATERFORD

9

SHU
BELFAST, NORTHERN IRELAND

10

THE WATERMARGIN
BELFAST, NORTHERN IRELAND

AN CARN

Deuglán & Siobhán O Réagáin
Ring, Dungarvan,
Co Waterford
Tel: (058) 46611, Fax: 46614
ancarn@eircom.net
www.ancarn.com

Another fantastic addition to the riches of the West Waterford scene, An Carn is an archetypal him'n'her restaurant.

An Carn is set high and handsome up the steep hill of Ring, in the Irish-speaking Gaeltacht area of West Waterford, an enchanting place. And enchantment is just what Deuglán and Siobhán O'Réagáin aim to achieve with their delicious cooking in this pretty restaurant with rooms. Their youthful enthusiasm is abetted by a culinary maturity that creates impressively flavourful and decisively imaginative food: lovely spiced turnip and sweetcorn chowder; seared smoked salmon with honey, mustard and dill cream; local mussels with garlic and crisp breadcrumbs; lemon and black pepper chicken on boxty; and the fish and meat cookery all has delightful, considered nuances, such as a fruity basil oil with hake, or a rich balsamic jus with sirloin. Mrs O'Réagáin's desserts are fabulous classics: sticky toffee pudding; chocolate roulade; a splendid Bailey's delice gateau. Enchanting.

- **OPEN:** July & Aug Tue-Sun 6.30pm-9.30pm, Sep-June Thur-Sun 6.30pm-9.30pm. Closed 2 wks Mar, 1 wk Sep
- **PRICE:** Dinner €30, House wine €15.35
- **CREDIT CARDS:** Visa, Mastercard, Diners

- **NOTES:**
Full wheelchair access. Children welcome. Four guest bedrooms, one fully wheelchair friendly.

- **DIRECTIONS:**
Take the Cork road out of Dungarvan for 2 miles. Turn left for Ring. Follow signposts for An Carn, 1km up the hill from Mooney's pub.

BUGGY'S GLENCAIRN INN

Ken & Cathleen Buggy
Glencairn, nr Lismore,
Co Waterford
Tel: (058) 56232, Fax: 56232
buggysglencairninn@eircom.net
www.lismore.com

So, what's to love in Buggy's? Well, everything, starting with the chips.

Ken and Cathleen Buggy's Glencairn Inn may look the very picture of a postcard-pretty country village, with images borrowed from a painting by Constable, as devised by an advertising agency. But what makes Buggy's unique - and there really is no other word for it - is the fact that Ken and Cathleen Buggy are so utterly, inimitably, unclichéd. No advertising agency could concoct a couple like this. The way they cook, the way they decorate their lovely Inn, creates a place which has no equivalent in Ireland. The wit and originality they bring to their work, to decoration, to cooking, to serving food and wine and drinks, gives the Glencairn Inn a Bohemianism you will find nowhere else. As a cook, Mr Buggy is a free spirit, weaving influences from everywhere into his own fusion of flavours. His fish cookery is sublime, his chips the best you can eat, his breakfasts a marvel. Unique is right.

● **OPEN:** From 7.30pm-9pm, booking essential
● **PRICE:** Dinner €33, House wine €16.40
● **CREDIT CARDS:** Visa, Mastercard

● **NOTES:**
Closed weekdays off season, and 23 Dec-10 Jan.
No Wheelchair access. No smoking in bedrooms.
No facilities for children.

● **DIRECTIONS:**
In Lismore turn right at the monument, go to Horneybrook's garage, there is a sign to Glencairn. Follow this road for 3 miles, until you come to the Inn.

POWERSFIELD HOUSE

Eunice Power & Edmund Power
Ballinamuck West,
Dungarvan, Co Waterford
Tel: (058) 45594, Fax: 45550
powersfieldhouse@cablesurf.com
www.powersfield.com

Ask not how Eunice does all she does, just be grateful and appreciative for all she does.

Eunice Power is a mighty cook, and a meticulous restaurateur. Everything in Powersfield House gleams and shows great care, the perfect canvas for this spirited cook to show just what she can do.

First off, she can write a menu that makes you want to eat everything on offer. When you finally choose - opting for rarities such as piadina, or roast aubergine soup, or salmon and mussels poached in a Thai broth - the food impresses as deeply considered, and utterly delicious. That piadina with goat's cheese and grilled peppers is just knockout, the aubergine soup is sharpened with a twist of lime, and a main course of fillet steak with onion and marmalade and champ is a riot of flavour, some of the best meat cookery you will eat in Ireland. Sticky pear and ginger cake and lemon tart are benchmark, and that is the only way to describe Powersfield: benchmark.

- **OPEN:** 7pm-10pm Thu-Sat
- **PRICE:** Dinner €36, House wine €18.50
- **CREDIT CARDS:** All major cards accepted

- **NOTES:**
Full wheelchair access.
Children welcome with notice, if supervised.

- **DIRECTIONS:**
Take the Clonmel/Cappoquin road from Dungarvan, and the house is the second turn to the left, and the first house on the right.

RICHMOND HOUSE

Paul & Claire Deevy
Cappoquin, Co Waterford
Tel: (058) 54278, Fax: 54988
info@richmondhouse.net
www.richmondhouse.net

Richmond may well be serving the finest country house cooking you will find in Ireland.

Paul Deevy may be cooking the finest country house cuisine you can find in Ireland right now. Ably assisted by his lieutenant, Maria Wall, Mr Deevy's cooking has a quiet confidence, and a winningly understated panache, He loves the wild flavours of rabbit - roasted and served with a confit of tomatoes and melting mozzarella - of pheasant - wrapped in bacon and served with honey roast carrots - and his trademark West Waterford lamb - served with braised lentils. Fish and shellfish get the sublime Richmond treatment - prawns with ketaifi pastry; cod with celeriac purée. Mr Deevy also cooks one of the most excellent vegetarian menus you will find, a gesture which is typical of his generosity and thoughtfulness. This is great cooking, delightfully served by Claire Deevy and her team, and there is nowhere nicer to eat it than in the comfort of Richmond.

● **OPEN:** Open for dinner Mon-Sun (closed Sun off season)
● **PRICE:** Dinner €43, House wine €18
● **CREDIT CARDS:** Visa, Mastercard, Amex, Diners

● **NOTES:**
Recommended for vegetarians, and delighted to cater for coeliac and vegans with advance notice. Wheelchair access with assistance. Children welcome.

● **DIRECTIONS:**
Just outside the town of Cappoquin, and well signposted from the road.

THE TANNERY RESTAURANT

Paul and Máire Flynn,
10 Quay St, Dungarvan,
Co Waterford
Tel: (058) 45420, Fax: 45518
tannery@cablesurf.com
www.tannery.ie

The most thoughtful cook
and the most thoughtful
– and delicious – cooking
in Ireland.

In the beautiful and elegant restaurant space that is The Tannery, Paul Flynn conjures some of the most original cookery to be found in contemporary Irish cuisine.

Where others look overseas for inspiration, Mr Flynn has returned to his roots, to the agrestic and domestic Irish foods of his childhood. He will cook a tournedos of pork, for instance - a little-used cut from the neck - to produce a dish so artful, that you feel you have never eaten true pork before. And this skill is used with every dish: homecorned beef with buttered spring cabbage; superlative rum and raisin pannacotta; brilliant warm gingerbread with maple syrup. Mr Flynn is the most cerebral of Irish cooks, and yet he cooks in the most ancient way: slowly, curing and braising, simmering and poaching, making his own time with everything, and that beatific patience pervades every aspect of The Tannery.

- **OPEN:** Lunch Tue-Fri & Sun, Dinner Tue-Sat
- **PRICE:** Dinner €36, House wine €17.20
- **CREDIT CARDS:** Visa, Mastercard, Amex, Diners

- **NOTES:**
Full wheelchair access. Children welcome lunchtime and early evening. Private dining room to cater for parties up to 30.

- **DIRECTIONS:**
At the end of Lower Main Street, to the right of the old Market House Building.

WHITE HORSES

**Christine Power &
Geraldine Flavin
Main Street
Ardmore,
Co Waterford
Tel: (024) 94040**

A dreamy little seaside restaurant that seems as if it has appeared out of some movie spooling in your imagination.

Sisters Christine and Geraldine - the former minding front of house, the latter minding the stoves - have created an idyllic little restaurant in White Horses, just the sort of place you might dream of finding in a frothy little resort town like Ardmore. Dream no more: here it is.

It's a simple, L-shaped room, with a little counter which displays the delightful cakes, bakes and desserts baked that morning, one of the restaurant's great attractions.

But the savoury cooking also has imagination and expertise: crab toes with dill béarnaise; chicken kebab with root ginger and mushroom; seared scallops with asparagus and baby corn, all the way to riches and richness such as lobster thermidor or grilled sirloin with brandy and pepper butter. The cooking and the ambience of White Horses are very personal, very feminine, the work of talented women whose care shines through.

● **OPEN:** 11am-11pm Tue-Sun (winter opening 11am-11pm Fri & Sat, 11am-6pm Sun) Closed January
● **PRICE:** Lunch €10-18, Dinner €20, House wine €15.50
● **CREDIT CARDS:** Visa, Mastercard

● **NOTES:**
Wheelchair access.
Children welcome, high chair.

● **DIRECTIONS:**
In the centre of the village, which is off the N25, about 7 miles from Youghal.

10 RESTAURANTS
WITH GREAT MUSIC

1

ALDEN'S
BELFAST, NORTHERN IRELAND

2

THE CUSTOMS HOUSE
BALTIMORE, CO CORK

3

DISH
DUBLIN, CO DUBLIN

4

GINGER
BELFAST, NORTHERN IRELAND

5

HALO
DUBLIN, CO DUBLIN

6

JACQUES
CORK, CO CORK

7

THE MERMAID
LISCANNOR, CO CLARE

8

THE MERMAID CAFÉ
DUBLIN, CO DUBLIN

9

SHANAHAN'S
DUBLIN, CO DUBLIN

10

TRIBECA
DUBLIN, CO DUBLIN

THE WINE VAULT

David Dennison
High Street, Waterford,
Co Waterford
Tel: (051) 853444, Fax: 853777
bacchus@eircom.net
www.waterfordwinevault.com

David Dennison's classic wine bar and cellar is the Waterford city destination for food and wine lovers.

The Wine Vault is one of those rooms where it is always a pleasure to push open the door, pull up a seat, order a bottle and peruse the menu one more time. Like a comfortable coat or a favourite pair of shoes, it is familiar, welcoming, understated and always attractive. Nice to be back, you say to yourself.

David Dennison and his team have a professional demeanour, a smartness and alertness which have powered this handsome room since the day it opened. They manage the task of serving good modern food in a clubable room along with the business of a wine shop with ease. Everything they do is underscored with thoughtfulness and a sangfroid which is very winning. the cooking has an easy deliciouness and composure which matches the serenity of the space, and all told this is one of the most distinctive addresses in the country.

- **OPEN:** 12.30pm-2.30pm, 5.30pm-10.30pm Mon-Sat (Sat closed 11pm)
- **PRICE:** Lunch €14-16, Dinner €35-30, House wine €19
- **CREDIT CARDS:** Visa, Mastercard, Amex

- **NOTES:**
Wheelchair access. Children welcome.

- **DIRECTIONS:**
Come up the quays, look for Ulster Bank, turn up towards City Square car park, go left, the Wine Vault is on the right.

THE LEFT BANK BISTRO

Annie McNamara & Mary McCullagh
Fry Place, Athlone,
Co Westmeath
Tel: (0902) 94446, Fax: 94598
mail@leftbankbistro.com
www.leftbankbistro.com

The true spirit of the rive gauche – in the very centre of the country – thanks to Annie and Mary.

Serendipity creates the things that we would never dare imagine, like the fact that the new home of the famed Left Bank Bistro is in Fry Place. Imagine! Even Skillet Street, or Wok Lane, could scarcely be more appropriate. The Left Bank Bistro, Fry Place, Athlone. Now, that's an address. You couldn't dream it up.

Nor could you dream up the success story that the LBB has become in Athlone, or its ever-increasing improvement over the years, or the devotion of its clientele to their great signature dish – tandoori chicken on focaccia (now, is that fusion or what?). This is a great room with great food, and it proudly wears the stylishness and confidence of the proprietors with gleeful bashfulness. Annie and Mary understand the Bohemianism and boisterousness and affability that makes for a great restaurant, and with great cooking, it's all in Fry Place.

- **OPEN:** From 10.30am Tue-Sat, lunch noon-5pm, dinner from 6pm.
- **PRICE:** Lunch €14.50, Dinner €35, House wine €17
- **CREDIT CARDS:** Visa, Mastercard, Amex

- **NOTES:**
Full wheelchair access.
Children welcome if supervised, no special menus, high chair.
No lunchtime reservations, booking advisable for dinner.

- **DIRECTIONS:**
In old Athlone, behind the castle.

WINEPORT LODGE

Jane English & Ray Byrne
Glasson, Athlone,
Co Westmeath
Tel: (0902) 85466, Fax: 85471
lodge@wineport.ie
www.wineport.ie

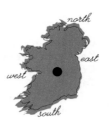

Wineport is one of the most revolutionary restaurants in Ireland, and with new rooms due to open, a new age beckons.

Ray Byrne and Jane English fly the flag for one of the forgotten crafts of the food business, that of the professional restaurateur.

Today, chefs dominate our thoughts about where we should eat, but Byrne and English show that smart restaurateurs – and there are no smarter restaurateurs than this pair – can actually be the most important and significant people in the restaurant operation. Various chefs have worked in the Wineport kitchens over the years, but it is to the Wineport style created by Ray and Jane that they all pay respect, and it is to the standards of delightful, contemporary Irish cooking established by the bosses that they must all find their measure.

The food is smart and delicious, the room is a pure joy, and new rooms which will open this year will see this hugely influential restaurant enter a new age, confident as ever.

- **OPEN:** Breakfast, lunch and dinner
- **PRICE:** Dinner €40, House wine €10
- **CREDIT CARDS:** All major cards accepted

- **NOTES:**
Full wheelchair access. Note rooms will be opening early in 2002, telephone for details.

- **DIRECTIONS:**
Take the Longford/Cavan exit off the Dublin/Galway road, fork left at the Dog and Duck pub, the Wineport Lodge is 1 mile further on on the left hand side.

LA MARINE

Bill Kelly
Kelly's Resort Hotel, Rosslare
Co Wexford
Tel: (053) 32114, Fax: 32222
kellyhot@iol.ie
www.kellys.ie

It seems that every dish is a signature dish in the hands of chef Eugene Callaghan.

La Marine Bistro, at Kelly's Hotel, has only been around for four years, but that has been all the time Eugene Callaghan has needed to create one of the most admired gourmet grottos in Ireland. It's a big, bold room, decorated with the sort of savvy that is evident in every detail of Kelly's Hotel, and it has been the perfect, bustling space for one of the most naturally gifted chefs in Ireland to show what he can do.

Just list the signature dishes: salt and pepper squid with soya and pickled ginger; pasta ribbons with asparagus, peas and home-dried tomatoes; Wexford mussels with garlic and pine nut crust; crispy duck confit; rib steak with gratin dauphinoise; Slaney river salmon with Parmesan-crusted fennel; pavlova with summer berries and chantilly cream. Logic, simplicity and culinary sureness come together here in food that is unpretentious and hugely enjoyable, a textbook example of modern Irish cooking. And don't miss the wine buff's wine list.

● **OPEN:** 12.30pm-2.30pm, 6.30pm-9.30pm Mon-Sun. Closed Dec-end Feb
● **PRICE:** Sun lunch €17.95, Lunch €21, Dinner €35, House wine €18
● **CREDIT CARDS:** All major cards accepted

● **NOTES:**
Wheelchair access with advance notice. Children welcome, high chair.

● **DIRECTIONS:**
Kelly's Hotel is well signposted from all roads in the area.

AVOCA

The Pratt family
Kilmacanogue, Co Wicklow
Tel: **(01) 286 7466**, Fax: **286 2376**
info@avoca.ie
www.avoca.ie

Avoca do the impossible. But it's the fact that they do it every day of the week that is amazing.

The impossible that Simon Pratt and his team accomplish each day is to satisfy thousands of people by serving them food that has true provenance, true flavour and true goodness. That sounds simple, but it proved beyond the capability of everyone before the Avoca team concentrated on creating the food culture that makes it happen every day of the week.

And that culture explains why the Avoca cafés are so superb; there is a true food culture evident in their work, an understanding, an experimentation, a sophistication that is simply magnificent. Others rely on systems; in Avoca they rely on knowledge, sympathy, nous. You can't make great food with systems, and the Avoca crew know this, and trust to instinct, and bloody hard work. The Avoca cafés are one of the glories of Ireland's contemporary food culture.

- **OPEN:** 9.30am-5.30pm Mon-Sun
- **PRICE:** Lunch €8-12
- **CREDIT CARDS:** All major cards accepted

- **NOTES:**
Other recommended restaurants: Powerscourt House, Tel: (01) 204 6070; Suffolk Street, D2, Tel: (01) 677 4215. Full wheelchair access in Kilmacanogue only. Children welcome.

- **DIRECTIONS:**
Kilmacanogue is on the N1. For Powerscourt follow signs to the gardens, Suffolk St is in centre of Dublin.

THE STRAWBERRY TREE

Eoin & Bernard Doyle
Macreddin Village, Aughrim,
Co Wicklow
Tel: (0402) 36444, Fax: 36580
brooklodge@macreddin.ie
www.brooklodge.com

Yeah, that's a pop star at the next table. Aren't they always smaller than you reckoned?

From the outside, it seems too planned and perfect. A purpose built hotel and restaurant, The Brook Lodge Inn and its Strawberry Tree Restaurant, is carved out of a green field site, exactly one hour south of Dublin's Donnybrook church. But you would be wrong. For here is a restaurant with a menu devoted to wild and organic foods, and a place where the kitchen team do everything they can to overturn any expectation of "hotel" food. The 'Tree is a place for creative cooking: wild rabbit comes with wild mushroom risotto and rich thyme and red wine gravy; monkfish is wrapped in dilisk seaweed and served with gently poached fennel; venison chops have a ruddy purée of swedes and roasted vegetables. It's smart, optimistic cooking with vivid flavours, the hotel itself is the chill-out capital of Wicklow, and the only calculation involved is in getting it right, night after night.

- **OPEN:** 7pm-9.30pm Mon-Sat, Sun lunch 1pm-7pm
- **PRICE:** Dinner €48, House wine €21
- **CREDIT CARDS:** All major cards accepted.

● **NOTES:**
Recommended for vegans, coeliacs and vegetarians. Full wheelchair access. Residents car park. Children welcome, babysitting, cots available.

● **DIRECTIONS:**
N11 Dublin to Rathnew, Co Wicklow. Right at r'about, on to Gleneally, on to Rathdrum. 1mile outside Rathdrum, right towards Aughrim via Ballinaclash.

THE TREE OF IDLENESS

Susan Courtellas
Sea Front, Bray,
Co Wicklow
Tel: (01) 286 3498
Fax: 282 8183

Ancient, elemental flavours that cannot be found anywhere else in Ireland are the trademark of the Tree.

The cooking in Susan Courtellas' Tree of Idleness remains as ancient and elementally pleasing as it has been throughout The Tree's long history. The flavours here are the undistilled ones of Greek-Cypriot cooking: melitzanosalata, the salad of aubergine with feta, olive oil, lemon juice and herbs; arni kapnisto, smoked best end of lamb; imam bayildi; quails maavrodaphne. There is a haute cuisine polish to the presentation of the food, but the flavours are as ancient as the Mediterranean, and in a restaurant world obsessed with newness, it is almost a shock to eat this food. Three other great attributes complete the capacious shade of hospitality. The dessert trolley is so extraordinary it is a treat unto itself. The wine list is one of the finest (and best value) in Ireland, and service - from Mrs Courtellas and manager Tom Monaghan - is delightful.

- **OPEN:** From 7.30pm Tue-Sun
- **PRICE:** Dinner €35-40, House wine €20
- **CREDIT CARDS:** Visa, Mastercard, Amex

- **NOTES:**
Wheelchair access, but not toilets.
Children welcome if well behaved.

- **DIRECTIONS:**
On the sea front, towards Bray Head.

NORTHERN IRELAND

ALDEN'S

Jonathan Davis
229 Upper Newtownards Rd
Belfast BT4 3JF
Tel: (028) 9065 0079,
Fax: 9065 00332

Not many restaurants manage
to have all the virtues,
but Alden's seems to be one
that does.

Some cooks are so good that you can find yourself asking;
is there anything they can't cook to perfection?

After numerous meals at Alden's, you ask this about Cath
Gradwell. Isn't there a chink anywhere in that capacious
culinary armour? How can she cook roast leg of rabbit
with cotechino sausage, lentils and salsa verde as
resplendently as fillet of salmon with hollandaise and
chips. How can red pepper and feta mousse be just as fab
as vegetable risotto with rocket and goat's cheese, or
those incredible desserts: rhubarb granita with apple
brandy; grilled pineapple with chilli syrup.

Actually, there is hope for us mere mortals: Ms Gradwell
makes a decent curry with mushrooms, and it's good. But
it's not shatteringly delicious and divine, like everything
else is, so just skip the curries. Brilliant service, beautiful
room, one of the great destinations.

● **OPEN:** Noon-2.30pm Mon-Fri, 6pm-10pm Mon-Sat
(till 11pm Fri & Sat)
● **PRICE:** Lunch £15, Dinner £25, House wine £12.50
● **CREDIT CARDS:** All major cards accepted.

● **NOTES:**
Wheelchair access. Children welcome.

● **DIRECTIONS:**
Up on the Upper Newtownards Road, near the cross
roads with Sandown Road.

BELFAST BAR & GRILL

Paul Rankin's Belfast Bar & Grill
The Ramada Hotel
Shaw's Bridge, Belfast BT7 8XP
Tel: (028) 9092 3500
mail@ramadabelfast.com

Paul Rankin's BB&G is a startlingly funky new riff on so-called traditional Irish dishes.

The menu in the Belfast Bar & Grill reads like pastiche from Ireland's agricultural past - Irish stew; crubeens; potted duck; lamb with mint butter; custard tart; raspberry rice pudding - but rest assured that these dishes taste as contemporary as all get out. The reason why they are so cutting edge is thanks to the involvement of Paul Rankin. The BB&G allows Rankin to explore the possibility that Ireland's traditional foods are not simply a culinary relic, but can form part of the contemporary culinary argot. The food is dazzlingly successful: fish cake with poached egg; potted duck with superb Donegal chutney; fish and chips with mushy peas. Local icon foods are used wisely: Black Bush in a warm chocolate cake; Guinness in a creamy sauce with venison; Walter Ewing's salmon; Strangford Lough oysters. Rankin's achievement is a mighty one: he has re-energised Irish traditional foods and made them new.

● **OPEN:** Noon-2.30pm Mon-Fri, noon-3pm Sun, 6pm-10pm Mon-Thur, 6pm-10.30pm Fri-Sat
● **PRICE:** Lunch £15.50, Dinner £20, House wine £13.50
● **CREDIT CARDS:** Visa, Mastercard, Amex

● **NOTES:**
Full wheelchair access. Children welcome, high chair, menu. Recommended for vegetarians.

● **DIRECTIONS:**
On the first floor of the hotel. Travel straight up the Malone Road to outer ring from where it is signposted.

CAYENNE

Paul & Jeanne Rankin
7 Lesley House,
Shaftesbury Square, Belfast BT2
Tel: (028) 9033 1532,
Fax: 90261575 reservations@
www.cayennerestaurant.com

Still the hippest kid on the block after all these years, Cayenne is glamorous, and ageing as well as Deneuve.

Cayenne is glam and funky, the John Galliano of the Belfast restaurant scene. Best of all, it's not self-conscious: it's a hip trip, not a nervous one, a great date restaurant, not a vanity project, a cool joint which is accessible to all. Paul and Jeannie Rankin managed the virtually impossible when they changed livery from the much-loved Roscoff, but their recognition that change was vital was perceptive and smart. They changed as seamlessly as Andy Warhol moving from genre to genre. They simplified the food, making it more cutting-edge and yet approachable. It's fusion in style - seafood risotto perfumed with Thai green curry; salmon with lemongrass and lime crème fraiche; char-grilled squid with chorizo and rocket - but the kitchen's control is impressive. Desserts are outstanding - pear and chocolate pound cake; fantastic honeycomb ice cream. The Rankins understand cool, simple as that.

● **OPEN:** Noon-2.30pm Mon-Fri, 6pm-11.15pm Mon-Sat
● **PRICE:** Lunch £10.50, Dinner £25, House wine £13.75
● **CREDIT CARDS:** All major cards accepted

● **NOTES:**
Wheelchair access. Children welcome. Recommended for vegetarians and special diets.

● **DIRECTIONS:**
Belfast city centre, overlooking Shaftesbury Square.

RESTAURANT MICHAEL DEANE

Michael Deane
38-40 Howard Street,
Belfast BT1 PD
Tel: (028) 90331134
deanesbelfast@deanesbelfast.com
www.deanesbelfast.com

Dining in the grand
baroque style, but Michael
Deane's cooking is modern
and original.

Deane's is two eating places; a downstairs brasserie which is still struggling to find consistency since chef Ray McArdle moved on, and the baroque-styled upstairs dining room where chef-patron Michael Deane himself cooks between Wednesday and Saturday evenings.

The formality of the room and the service is rather out of step with the way in which people eat in modern Ireland – it's very much a take on that old warhorse, "fine dining" a concept we have never understood – but Michael Deane's cooking is as hip-to-the-trip as anyone's, and his signature style of fusing Asian elements with French classical influences is utterly convincing. In fact, no one does them as well as this chef: an open pasta of roasted scallops with velouté of Jerusalem artichokes; confit of aubergine with goat's cheese; wild creations such as fillet of beef with lemongrass mash and haggis.

● **OPEN:** 7pm-9.30pm Wed-Sat, 12.15pm-2pm Fri
● **PRICE:** Lunch, £19.50, Dinner £38.50, House wine £15
● **CREDIT CARDS:** All major cards accepted.

● **NOTES:**
No wheelchair access to restaurant. No children.

● **DIRECTIONS:**
Near the City Hall in Belfast city centre. Upstairs, over Deane's Brasserie.

THE DUKE RESTAURANT

**Ciaran Gallagher
The Duke Restaurant,
The Duke Bar, Duke Street,
Warrenpoint, BT34 3JY
Tel: (028) 4175 2084
www.dukerestaurant.com**

Duke's has hoovered up all
the local trade way down south,
and it's easy to see how
and why.

Ciaran Gallagher is serious about his cooking, but he has no pretensions, and this explains why Duke's (which you will find above Duke's Pub) is a runaway success. He will offer the chicken Marylands and the surf'n'turf stuff for his cautious customers, but just turn the page to the special dishes and look what this man can really do: grilled turbot with wilted bak choi and prawn bisque cream; tuna loin with mango and spiced guacamole; lobster in brandy and cream; roast barramundi with lemon and basil risotto. Most chefs couldn't handle the strain of this schizophrenic division of food, but Gallagher takes it all in his stride, and packs in the happy punters. Essentially, Duke's succeeds because it gives you exactly what you want, rather than the situation in many restaurants where they offer you only what they feel like offering you. This is smart food, from an ambitious chef relishing his work.

- **OPEN:** 6pm-10pm (from 7pm) Tue-Sun
- **PRICE:** Dinner £18, House wine £8
- **CREDIT CARDS:** Visa, Mastercard

- **NOTES:**
No wheelchair access. Children welcome. Vegetarian 'surprise'.

- **DIRECTIONS:**
From Newry, 6miles on the A2. Just off the square in the centre of Warrenpoint, upstairs at the Duke pub.

FONTANA

Colleen Bennett & Stephen McAuley
61a High Street, Holywood,
Co Down,
Tel: (028) 9080 9908,
info@fontanarestaurant.com
www.fontanarestaurant.com

Do the good people of Holywood know how lucky they are to have Fontana on their main street?

Anywhere else, Fontana would attract humungous amounts of attention for its searingly modern, confidently delicious cooking, But, standards are so high in Northern Ireland restaurants, it means that Colleen Bennett's restaurant doesn't get the sort of serious kudos that it richly deserves. So, let's put that right: Fontana is a great modern Irish restaurant, which enjoys all the merits of signature cooking, good prices, friendly service, the lot.

Maybe it's because the food is so simple and commonsensical that folk just take it for granted, but simplicity and commonsense are the constituents of culinary wisdom, and they know that here. Give us the veal loin with gremolata and a veal jus, or the salmon with wilted Chinese greens and a black bean vinaigrette, or the duck breast with thyme and red wine lentils, and we are happy campers. Great cooking, and a great restaurant.

- **OPEN:** Noon-2.30pm Mon-Sat, 5pm-9.30pm Mon-Sat (from 6.30pm-10pm Sat), 11am-3pm Sun brunch
- **PRICE:** Dinner £17.50, House wine £12
- **CREDIT CARDS:** Visa, Mastercard and Delta/Switch

- **NOTES:**
No wheelchair access, but staff happy to assist up the stairs. Disabled toilet upstairs. Children welcome, but no special menu. Recommended for vegetarians. Special diets catered for with style.

- **DIRECTIONS:**
The entrance is down an alleyway, between the opticians and interior design shop on the High Street.

GINGER

Simon McCance
217 Ormeau Rd,
Belfast,
Northern Ireland
BT7 3GG
Tel: (028) 9049 3143

Shoe-string minimalism and zippideedoodah cooking is the mighty Ginger mix.

No menus. No tablecloths. No wine list. Bare walls decorated with the occasional picture of accordion players. Schwartz glass pepper grinders on the bare tables. Simon McCance considered calling his restaurant 'Food'. Well, maybe 'Minimalism' might have been on the list. Or 'Shoestring', perhaps?

McCance has his priorities right. Ginger is about his cooking and nothing else, save perhaps a cool James Brown soundtrack that shows he has his soul priorities right. McCance likes savoury flavours: warm smoked salmon with roast tomato and lentil dressing; his trademark crab salad with mango and a little light mayo, and even offers fillet of beef with chips as a starter. Rare breed pork with root vegetables and balsamic butter is punchy and polished; and hake with roast aubergine and garlic potatoes is just right. Great value, great service, great sounds, great place.

- **OPEN:** 5pm-9.30pm Tue-Sat, noon-3pm Sat
- **PRICE:** Lunch £3-£8, Dinner £20
- **CREDIT CARDS:** Visa, Mastercard

- **NOTES:**
Bring your own wine. Limited wheelchair access (no access to toilet). Children welcome.

- **DIRECTIONS:**
On the south side of the river, 200 yards from the bridge, on your right coming from the city centre.

10 RESTAURANTS
FOR STYLE LOVERS

1

BALLYNAHINCH CASTLE
CONNEMARA, CO GALWAY

2

L'ECRIVAIN
DUBLIN, CO DUBLIN

3

HALO
DUBLIN, CO DUBLIN

4

MULCAHY'S
KENMARE, CO KERRY

5

O'CALLAGHAN-WALSHE
ROSSCARBERY, CO CORK

6

ONE PICO
DUBLIN, CO DUBLIN

7

PORCELAIN
BELFAST, NORTHERN IRELAND

8

THE STRAWBERRY TREE
MACREDDIN, CO WICKLOW

9

THE TEA ROOM
DUBLIN, CO DUBLIN

10

ZUNI
KILKENNY, CO KILKENNY

NICK'S WAREHOUSE

Nick & Kathy Price
35-39 Hill Street, Belfast
BT12 LB
Tel: (028) 9043 9690, Fax: 9023 0514
nicks@warehouse.dnet.co.uk
www.nickswarehouse.co.uk

Restaurant, wine bar and Anix, the pioneering Nick's Warehouse in Belfast's Cathedral quarter is all things to all men.

Nick's is virtually all things to all men: smart upstairs restaurant for lunchtime dining; wine bar for raucous fun; 200-square-foot Anix for casual eating and drinking. It's an ambitious and hugely successful trio – the sheer number of folk packed in here at weekends almost beggars belief – and whilst this pressure can impact on the consistency of the cooking at times, Nick's remains a key destination. Nick and Kathy Price were pioneers when they moved into the Cathedral Quarter back in 1989, but then they were pioneers long before that, as anyone who remembers their excellent cooking way, way back in Daft Eddie's on Sketrick Island will attest. Their menus still push at new discoveries all the time – laksa is likely to be alongside 80's dishes such as vegetarian crumble or pasta with baby corn, spinach and tomato – but it is the dishes which use artisan Norn Iron produce that work the best.

- **OPEN:** Noon-3pm Mon-Fri, 6pm-9.30pm Tue-Sat
- **PRICE:** Lunch downstairs £13.25, Lunch upstairs £21.50, Dinner £22.50, House wine £11.50
- **CREDIT CARDS:** Visa, Mastercard, Diners, Amex

- **NOTES:**
Wheelchair access downstairs. Children not permitted in the bar area after 9pm (NI licensing law).

- **DIRECTIONS:**
Nick's is situated near the back of St Anne's Cathedral, access is by way of Talbot Street, which runs down the side of the Cathedral.

ORIEL OF GILFORD

Barry Smyth
2 Bridge St, Gilford, Co Down
BT63 6HF
Tel: (028) 3883 1543
orielrestaurant@aol.com
www.orielrestaurant.com

Barry Smyth cooks with a wisdom and a modesty well beyond his years. Thank heavens, says mid-Ulster.

He is a nice bloke, young Barry Smyth, thoughtful, professional, and calm, a vital antidote to those chefs who believe that mania and macho are the key ingredients for a successful kitchen.

Along with sous chef Damian Tumilty, Mr Smyth cooks measured, composed and well-conceived food in the neat, way-out-of-the-way Oriel, at Gilford, food that accommodates his somewhat conservative clientele whilst at the same time chiding them along gently in the direction of new tastes and temptations; seared trout with gribiche sauce, or collops of monkfish with saffron beurre blanc are neat twists on familiar dishes; loin of lamb with pesto crust, or duck breast with carrotes vichy, are smart slants on classic flavours. Such subtle intelligence has won The Oriel a devoted following, wise folk who know a good thing when they eat it.

- **OPEN:** 12.30pm-2.30pm Tue-Fri & Sun, 5pm-9.30pm Tue-Sat. Closed Mon.
- **PRICE:** Dinner stg£26.95, House wine £10.95-13.95
- **CREDIT CARDS:** Visa, Mastercard, Access, Switch, Solo, Amex

- **NOTES:**
Wheelchair access to all areas except Gents. No facilities for children. Recommended for vegetarians.

- **DIRECTIONS:**
On the road between Portadown and Banbridge. Go straight ahead at the mini roundabout, heading for Armagh.

PORCELAIN

Paul & Nicholas Hill
Ten Square, 10 Donegall Sq,
Belfast, BT1 5JD
Tel: (028) 9024 1001
Fax: 90243210 mail@ten-sq.com
www.ten-sq.com

Knife; fork; chopsticks; here's the new fusion in all its handsome international livery.

Glamorous and serene, Porcelain sets out its fusion food stall straight away: knife and fork are there on the table, and chopsticks too. Welcome to the new Belfast. Chef Niall McKenna (no relation, folks, as far as we know) pushes the fusion note further than anyone else has dared, so there is seared spicy pork belly with Napa slaw, fillet of beef with Japanese horseradish and parsley gratin, sea bass with somen noodles with an asparagus and truffle dressing.

Done wrong, this food is a travesty. Done right, it's a treat: light and nervy flavours such as field greens salad with sashimi, or seared rare tuna with Sichuan pepper, or rock shrimp tempura. The alert flavours of mirin and soy dance around the dishes, yielding to sumptuous desserts such as chocolate and raspberry Christion or warm chocolate and nut samosas with pistachio ice cream. Porcelain is radical, and the rooms in Ten Square create a great destination.

- **OPEN:** 8am-10am, noon-3pm, 6pm-11pm Mon-Sat (last orders 10.30pm Mon-Wed)
- **PRICE:** Lunch £10.95, Dinner £30
- **CREDIT CARDS:** Visa, Mastercard, Amex

- **NOTES:**
Wheelchair access. Children welcome. China club members bar.

- **DIRECTIONS:**
Opposite the back entrance of Belfast's City Hall, in the very centre of the city.

SHANKS

Robbie & Shirley Millar
The Blackwood,
150 Crawfordsburn Rd, Clandeboye,
Bangor, BT19 1GB
Tel: (028) 9185 3313, Fax: 9185 2493
www.shanksrestaurant.com

The most beautiful food in the most beautiful restaurant building in the country.

It's kind of easy to take Shanks for granted right now, what with Robbie and Shirley Millar being household names and media figures in the North, and Shanks' reputation as one of the great Irish restaurants effortlessly forged in gold.

But back when it opened, and when people first saw this radical O'Donnell and Twomey building and first ate Millar's searingly brilliant food, Shanks was seriously at risk of being in the wrong place at the wrong time. Starred food in the most modern building in Northern Ireland in the middle of a public golf course? Come on!

What made it all work, aside from the architectural brilliance, was the sheer brilliance of the food, and the benchmark service. Millar has a style all his own, and a collection of signature dishes the envy of every chef. The room is sublime, the service as good as it gets. Awesome.

- **OPEN:** 12.30pm-2.30pm Tue-Fri, 7pm-10pm Tue-Sat
- **PRICE:** Lunch £21, Dinner £38, House wine £16.50
- **CREDIT CARDS:** Visa, Mastercard, Amex

- **NOTES:**
Wheelchair access. Recommended for vegetarians. Children welcome, high chair, menu.

- **DIRECTIONS:**
Situated in the Blackwood Golf Centre, just off the main Belfast to Bangor road.

SHU

Alan Reid
253 Lisburn Rd, Belfast BT9 7EN
Tel: (028) 9038 1655,
Fax: 9068 1632
eat@shu-restaurant.com
www.shu-restaurant.com

The food may be crazily eclectic, but Shu works, and has one of the hippest audiences you can find.

Most chefs would despair of making the menu at Shu work. Here is everything from salt cod fritters to spiced chickpea casserole to sushi to omelette Arnold Bennett, a series of choices that suggests madness rather than a considered eclecticism.

And yet, it all works, and not only works, but works well, and consistently. You can actually order with complete confidence in Shu, with your date having the hake with Asian greens and green curry whilst you have the duck confit with Asian broth, before you enjoy caramelised lemon tart or bread and butter pudding, and it is the individual precision of the dishes which amazes, the fact that there is no gratuitous experimentation, but instead a true search to make each dish a success.

Such consistency has won a very, very stylish audience, so Shu demands your Blahniks and Paul Smith.

● **OPEN:** 12.30pm-2.30pm Mon-Fri, 7pm-10pm Mon-Sat
● **PRICE:** Lunch £12, Dinner £23-25, House wine £12.50
● **CREDIT CARDS:** Visa, Mastercard, Amex

● **NOTES:**
Wheelchair access. Children welcome, high chair.

● **DIRECTIONS:**
At the lower end of the Lisburn Road, opposite Windsor Avenue.

SMYTH'S

Alison & Aylmer Smyth
The Diamond
2-4 Lever Rd, Portstewart
Co L'derry BT55 7EF
Tel: (028) 7083 3564, Fax: 7083 5551
smythsrestaurant@aol.com

A new destination address for the north east coast, Smyth's is imaginative and adventurous.

Alison and Aylmer Smyth returned from England to create Smyth's restaurant from Mr Smyth's old home in Portstewart, bringing with them an ambitious attitude and a desire to create a restaurant centred around real cooking and good hospitality. As design consultants, they had little problem getting the interior right, but they also pulled together the food and service in double-quick time, which meant Smyth's has been making waves ever since it opened.

The cooking is smart and enjoyable: mushroom pâté en croûte or their savoury cheesecake with Cashel Blue are pretty, painterly – if slightly heavy – starters, mains are solid senders of meaty flavours: lamb with mint, garlic and chilli, Angus beef with chicken liver pâté, and they even serve the classic – and much neglected – steak garni, here called the steak dinner. A key new address.

- **OPEN:** Noon-3pm, 5.30pm-10.30pm (closed 8.30pm Sun) Brasserie and bar snacks available over extended hours during the summer.
- **PRICE:** Lunch £11, Dinner £20-25, House wine £8.99
- **CREDIT CARDS:** Visa, Mastercard

- **NOTES:**
Children welcome, menu, high chair and baby changing. Nursing mothers welcome. Sunday is family day. Wheelchair access downstairs, but not toilets.

- **DIRECTIONS:**
On the Diamond in the centre of town.

THE SUN KEE

Peter Lo
28 Donegal Pass,
Belfast BT7
Northern Ireland
Tel: (028) 9031 2016

To hell with good manners: no way are you sharing anything with anyone in the SK.

Edmund Lau has departed the Sun Kee and opened The Water Margin down the street, but everyone's favourite Chinese restaurant has continued serving the most sensational Chinese food without a blip in consistency and quality. A single little room which will frequently be packed with Belfast's Chinese community, the Sun Kee is the very definition of a cult destination. You bring your own booze, the food is riotously cheap, the craic mighty. Everything is good, but the chef's specialities are exceptional: bah won chicken breast; perfect Cantonese roast duck; the fab beef flank; the immortal char siu and monkfish in batter. Everyone loves this amiable place, none more so than the assorted chefs of Belfast, who will be competing with you in the queue to get a table. Just elbow them out of the way: the food here is too good for you to demonstrate any decorum or politesse.

- **OPEN:** 5pm-11pm Mon-Sun (closed Friday)
- **PRICE:** Dinner from £15
- **CREDIT CARDS:** No credit cards

- **NOTES:**
Bring your own wine. Full takeaway menu. Wheelchair access. Children welcome.

- **DIRECTIONS:**
Beside the police station on Donegal Pass.

LE TAVOLE

Johnnie Ritchie
479-481 Lisburn Road
Belfast,
BT9 7EZ
Tel: (028) 9066 3211
Fax: 9068 7304

A new top-notch neighbourhood restaurant with real Mediterranean flavours.

Everyone talks about the Mediterranean diet, but in Le Tavole you can actually taste it, in all it's clear-eyed deliciousness. Johnnie Ritchie and his devoted team have the chops and the understanding to make this simple but demanding food actually work. Warm salad of poached salt cod with potatoes, peas and a Greek walnut pesto, and seared rare roast beef with Manchego cheese, sweet pickled onion and olives, show the sort of serious understanding this team possess, whilst rustic fare such as lamb shank with garlic and parsley mash and a roast red pepper and tomato sauce, or grilled poussin with wild mushroom and barley risotto, take the examples of the Med and give them delicious, vibrant life. Some aspects of the service and housekeeping need to be attended to, but, for a novice, Le Tavole has attitude and ability in perfectly judged measure.

- **OPEN:** Noon-3.30pm, 6pm-10pm Tue-Sat
- **PRICE:** Lunch £4.95, Dinner £17, House wine £7.95
- **CREDIT CARDS:** Visa, Mastercard

- **NOTES:**
No wheelchair access. Children welcome.

- **DIRECTIONS:**
On the right hand side of the Lisburn Road, if heading away from the city centre, opposite the very large police station.

THE WATERMARGIN

Edmund Lau
The Water Margin
159-161 Donegall Pass
Belfast, BT7 1DT
Tel: (028) 9032 6888

You want the queer gear?
They've got it here! Walk on
the wild side of the water
margin.

The Water Margin is the wildest walk on the wild side
you will find in Ireland. You seek shark's fin and meat soup
dumplings? Fish head in black bean sauce? Ox tripe with
turnip? Marinated duck web and feet? Frog's legs with
bitter melon? Crispy fried pork intestine? Then walk into
this elegantly converted old church, at the Ormeau Road
end of Donegall Pass, and Edmund Lau and his team will
take you to that wild side of Chinese food, the echt
flavours and textures that can't be found anywhere else.
The Water Margin is huge, noisy, colourful, and packed
with the most delightful, helpful, friendly staff. If you don't
want the wild stuff, there is plenty of conventional
Chinese food also - the menu extends to 24 pages in
total! - so everyone manages to get just what they want.
This is a fabulous restaurant with no equivalent anywhere
else in Ireland. Don't miss it.

- ● **OPEN:** 9am-11.15pm Mon-Sun
- ● **PRICE:** Lunch £10, Dinner £20
- ● **CREDIT CARDS:** Visa, Mastercard

● **NOTES:**
Dim sun menu available 9am-5pm. Wheelchair access.
Children welcome.

● **DIRECTIONS:**
At the outer end of Donegall Pass, in a huge old
converted church, and hard to miss.

INDEX

Also from Estragon Press...

● In this provocative book, John McKenna offers a radical analysis of how restaurants operate, and why some restaurants succeed where others fail.

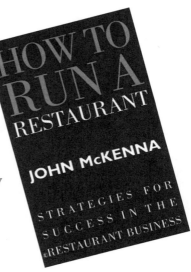

● Examining the business from the position of a customer and a critic, McKenna analyses the factors which contribute to success, and explores the decisions which have to be understood by anyone who is either already running a restaurant, or considering opening a new restaurant.

● Practitioners and students will find the book an exhilarating intellectual exploration of one of the most mercurial and fascinating industries and entertainments in the world.

The Bridgestone Guides on the web

To access up-to-the-minute information about Ireland's food culture, and to discover any changes or alterations that may have occurred with the entries in the Bridgestone guides, visit:

www.bridgestoneguides.com

As well as a monthly newsletter, **megabytes,** bridgestoneguides.com brings you up-to-date information on the entries in the Bridgestone 100 Best Guides, as well as a host of news on Irish food.

Go on line for the good news...

VISIT:
www.bridgestoneguides.com

The Bridgestone food lover's guides to Ireland:

The Traveller's Guide

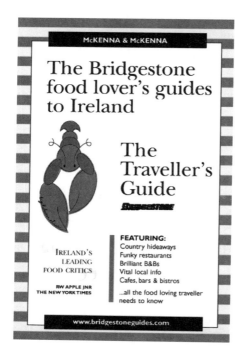

Here, in a single, compact volume is all the information the food lover needs to access the best places to eat and stay in Ireland. From the simplest pubs with real cooking, to the cutting edge of contemporary Irish cuisine, the Traveller's Guide will tell you the vital who, what and where throughout the highways and byways of Ireland.

The Bridgestone food lover's guides to Ireland:

The Shopper's Guide

With succinct wit and humour, the Shopper's Guide tells you who are the most important artisan producers in Ireland, and exactly where you can source and discover the fabulous foods they produce. If you want the inside track on Ireland's glorious food culture, you need to travel with the Shopper's Guide.

megabytes

is a fun, informative and up-to-the-minute e-zine written by John McKenna and a host of contributors, bringing you the vital news and views on the world of Irish and international food.

- **Restaurant reviews**

- **Seasonal recipes**

- **Reader's reports**

- **Campaigns to protect our food culture**

- **Competitions with great prizes**

- **Special offers**

- **A food lovers' noticeboard**

visit **bridgestoneguides.com** and sign up! It's completly free!

Other titles from Estragon Press...

The companion volume to this guide is The Bridgestone 100 Best Places to Stay:

Irish hospitality is justly celebrated, and here are the vital addresses and destinations for every food loving traveller.

The Bridgestone 100 Best Places to Stay in Ireland 2002 describes the finest country houses, B&B's and hotels that you can find in Ireland right now. This is the guide to lead you straight to the heart of one of the great cultures of hospitality in the world.